Traditional and Western Medicine

Traditional and Western Medicine

Voices from Jamaican Psychiatric Patients

CARYL JAMES BATEMAN

The University of the West Indies Press

Jamaica • Barbados • Trinidad and Tobago

DEDICATED TO ALL THOSE WHO CONTRIBUTED IN
MAKING THIS BOOK COME TO LIFE AND,
MOST OF ALL, TO THE STORYTELLERS WHO
GRACIOUSLY ALLOWED ME TO FIND A
HOME FOR YOUR STORIES.

The University of the West Indies Press
7A Gibraltar Hall Road, Mona
Kingston 7, Jamaica
www.uwipress.com

A catalogue record of this book is available from the
National Library of Jamaica.

ISBN: 978-976-640-845-9 (paper)
978-976-640-846-6 (Kindle)
978-976-640-847-3 (ePub)

Cover photograph by Mark Gentles
Cover and book design by Robert Harris
Set in Minion Pro 11/15 x 24

Printed in the United States of America

Contents

Figures

Introduction

THIS BOOK IS DESIGNED TO GIVE VOICE TO Jamaican psychiatric patients who are being treated in medical facilities in urban and rural Jamaica, that use Western biomedical approaches to treat mental illnesses (Lindo et al. 2006).

The work is based on research I conducted between 2005 and 2007 in pursuit of a doctorate in clinical psychology at the University of the West Indies, Mona, Jamaica. During this period, I operated between an urban hospital with psychiatric inpatients and outpatients, and a rural outpatient clinic at a rural hospital. The process outlined here is intended to assist others who have an interest in broadening their vision of the approach to treatment models, particularly as these relate to the use of traditional methods, alongside Western biomedical techniques.

Some 97 per cent of the population of Jamaica is of partial or total African descent (Encyclopedia of the Nations 2007). It is therefore understandable that psychiatric patients would hold on to their African heritage as this impacts on their experiences of their mental illness. Wedenoja (1983) has noted the paucity of literature on the culture of the people and their cultural worldview, beliefs and values. The African heritage has immediate relevance to how patients cope with their "behaviour, symptomology and psychodynamics" (Wedenoja 1983, 254–55). He implored researchers to examine folk healers, cults, sects and illness beliefs so as to better inform practice. A tension exists between the Western biomedical approach being used to treat psychiatric patients and the views of the patients who have an endemic belief in traditional rituals and cures that originate in Africa. My desire to understand patients' experiences on the ward and Wedenoja's imploration for more research to be done in the area, have been the driving force behind my journey.

The purpose of my work and therefore of this book, is to give voice to the patients' understanding of themselves as psychiatric patients in these urban and rural contexts. I value the patients' stories in uncovering this understanding, as only they can reveal the meanings of this lived experience. Grasping the themes that are present in their understanding is useful, as this information can be used to complement Western biomedicine and help us as practitioners to better meet the needs of the patients.

The stories of the six participants on whom the book focuses reflect the lived experience of their illnesses, in the context of the Western biomedical setting of the psychiatric ward and outpatient clinics at these two hospitals. I examine the patients' perception of their experiences and that of their practitioners. In becoming storytellers, the patients are finally given the opportunity to share their lived experiences of mental illness, allowing others to see what lies beyond the label of "major depressive, bipolar or a paranoid schizophrenic".

Chapter 1 highlights the background to the patients' perception of the experiences and the perception of the practitioners' experience of patients' illnesses. It gives a description of my journey as a researcher, gathering information from the storied lives of these participants and examining any gaps in the existing research by using the research questions I formulated. The reader will gain an understanding of the direction that I have decided to take. My quest is to be the narrator, giving voice to the patient's experiences, and through the use of hermeneutic phenomenology, learn about the intersubjective truth that exists between this narrator and the storyteller. The terms used throughout the research are operationalized so as to give clarity to the reader.

Chapter 2 consists of the extensive work that has been done in the area. It explores the position of the patient and that of the practitioner. In this chapter, I examine work done by other researchers that speak to the importance of highlighting the patients' understanding of their experiences and the value of listening to their stories. It examines how the historical and cultural beliefs in Western and traditional medicine can impact on the causes, explanation and treatment of mental illnesses. The relationship that psychiatric patients have had with Western and traditional medicine is examined. The work done in this chapter is placed within the theoretical framework of the Common-

Sense Model (Leventhal, Brissette and Leventhal 2003) and Goffman's (1959) theory of the total institution.

Chapter 3 gives an explanation of the different phases of the study from the first phase where I gain entry, to the final phase where I collect the data from both practitioners and patients. The quantitative approach marked only the beginning of the quest to further understand and uncover the truth, as it existed for each patient. The trends and major themes that emerge from the interviews are explained as well as any additional or unexpected themes which show up.

In chapter 4, I share the perspectives of sixty psychiatric patients regarding their specific diagnosis, what they believed the problem to be, whether or not it aligned with the treatment they received and what they were hoping to gain from the practitioners. This chapter also highlights thirty Western practitioners' views on traditional medicine and their perspectives on their patients' desire to speak about and access this type of care.

In chapter 5, I share in the intersubjective *truths* of the participants, exploring the true essences of their stories.

Finally, in chapter 6, the findings from both the quantitative (sixty psychiatric patients and thirty Western practitioners) and qualitative (six psychiatric patients) are triangulated and discussed as these relate to previous research in the area. The way forward is also presented.

The findings of this study are limited to the specific social and cultural contexts of Jamaican psychiatric wards and could not be generalized to other patients with other stages or types of disorders. As the patients were on the psychiatric ward, interviews had to be done in a timely manner when individuals were sufficiently cogent to participate. There were interviews that had to be discarded for several reasons, including the emotional and psychological state of the individuals while discussing issues that were difficult, the psychiatric routine, administration of medication, the discharge rates or patients not turning up for appointments, which meant that the interviews could not be completed. Also, some patients gave substantial information about the traditional mode of treatment but did not feel comfortable having this included in the study although they had signed an informed consent. The results were therefore limited in the number of patients that were included.

Because of the focus of the study and the scope of the data collected, the vignettes, open-ended questions and other qualitative data collected from the instruments were not included here as those fall beyond the scope of this study. They form part of another work.

CHAPTER 1

....

The Context of This Study

I BEGIN BY INTRODUCING YOU TO THE LIFEWORLD (*Lebenswelt*) of patients of the psychiatric ward, and to the ways in which I interacted with that world. I had viewed most of the days that I spent on the ward as a student in training as mundane. It was only when I was able to consciously experience my interactions with psychiatric patients that I came to a new understanding that this world contained rich information that, if uncovered, could inform practice. Understanding the patients' world would not have been possible without the combination of my discoveries from the quantitative findings of sixty patients and Western practitioners as well as hermeneutic phenomenological approaches used on my journey with the six key informants. In this chapter, I describe my experience with the psychiatric patients and my role as a researcher-practitioner.

Mondays through Fridays, my regular routine was to arrive at the hospital by 6:30 in the morning so that I could get an early start collecting my data. This process was now in its final stage and I only had a few participants left to interview. There was little activity early in the morning; the parking lot was practically empty, except for a few cars of the doctors or nurses who had been on night duty. I saw no one walking by. As I got out of my car, I immediately became aware of the voices of the patients coming from the psychiatric ward.

If there is anything that distinguishes this ward from others in the hospital, it is the loud and dramatic voices of the patients. From a distance, it was difficult to understand what was being said. The voices appeared to express a mixture of anger, frustration, confusion and happiness.

Although I had become used to hearing their clamour, by now I had come to appreciate them in a special way as I had gone through the process of data collection, and knew that if I took my time I could learn a lot from these very voices. I reached into the car for my books and the other research material I would need for the day, and approached the two-storey white building, painted the same colour as the rest of the hospital which is in need of renovation and modernization, designed as it was some sixty years before.

I structure each morning so that I can take the first hour to do some interviews before I go into my regular routine of seeing outpatients and attending classes. Inside the ward, on this morning, because of my habit of focusing on the floor while greeting the patients so as to avoid conversation, I am aware of the old black and white tiles. But today I have a different approach. I notice that I have been looking directly into the eyes of patients when I greet them as a few are participants in my study. Over time, my reaction to them gradually changed as I interviewed more patients and became familiar with the activities on the ward. I reach the landing before the staircase that leads to the second floor where we have classes. Today I am excited as I will be meeting with one of my participants, Dre. He always brings so much to his stories and is so patient with me in my attempts to understand his experiences. As I make my way up the staircase, the guard and three of the patients greet me with questions about their attending psychiatrist:

"Maanin Doc!" (Good morning, doctor)

"Wen mi ah go get release?" (When will I be released?)

"Yu see me psychiatris? Tell im seh me need fi see im." (Have you seen my psychiatrist? Tell him that I need to see him.)

This is customary, and as they await my response they continue holding on to the locked grille while peeking through the bars. In response to their questions I smile. I really do not have answers. I have no idea when they are going to be released, neither do I know who their psychiatrist is. By virtue of asking for "me psychiatris" these individuals are conforming to their roles as the mentally ill and therefore have become known as patients. The psychiatric lens views individuals who are behaving outside of the norms of society and are unable to function in their daily lives as mentally ill, and they are kept in this institution so as to regain normality (Goffman 1959).

The locked grille is symbolic. Only through its opening will the patient be released from this "total institution" (Goffman 1959) and, at the same time, it is the very thing he is holding on to. The guard and two other currently psychologically stable patients are sitting on the outside of the ward having been given permission to do so because they are much further along in their recovery.

It is not unusual for a psychologist in training such as myself to not know much about these patients' history as I have not had any opportunity to meet them outside of their psychiatric diagnosis. I have, however, had the opportunity to put aside my practitioner's lens and meet my participants as people. Throughout the study I have come to know three men and one woman who have been diagnosed with paranoid schizophrenia – Dre, Noel, Thomas, and Charlotte; and two women diagnosed with bipolar 1 with psychotic features – Fiona and Ariana. In sharing their storied lives, I have developed a relationship with each one, learned their names and personalities and have come to acknowledge that there is more to every participant than their diagnosis.

I am now no longer looking at the patients by the grille, but have started to look beyond them to see if I can identify any of my participants so that I can say hello. I feel that I have had a connection with each of the participants over the time they had taken to tell me about their lives. I am caught off-guard when one of the patients yells at me: "Look pan ar no. She look like she shoulda bi dung ere more dan we!" (Just look at her. She looks as if she ought to be here [on the ward] more than we do). The patients all begin laughing. I cannot help myself and begin laughing too as I find this statement funny. In the midst of my being preoccupied with my own thoughts, a patient is pointing out to me that by not maintaining eye contact I was showing the features of a mentally ill person. It is interesting how observant patients can be of the staff on the wards.

I finally see Charlotte. She is wearing blue denim pants and a purple top. Her medium-brown hair is unkempt and she is walking slowly in my direction. I am happy to see her, and I am about to greet her when I notice that she is looking past me. Her face is not as vibrant as it was when I first had my interview with her. She has little if any facial expression; her face is blank. It is almost as if I am not present in her world. This is confusing. I am saddened by the fact that she does not acknowledge me. She staggers across the walkway towards a plant, reaching out to it. She appears to be hallucinating. The fact that I have already established an empathetic bond with Charlotte increases my initial confusion. What I am observing does not match the Charlotte I had come to know. I cannot understand how this vibrant, confident person who shared so much with me in the past week appears so very different now. I continue up to the next landing at the top of the stairs, open the heavy glass doors, and as they shut tightly behind me the noises from the psychiatric ward below are locked away from my consciousness and from the ordered routine of graduate classes which would make up the rest of my day.

Later, when I begin to prepare for my interview with Dre, another participant, the experiences with Charlotte from the early morning are soon forgotten. Dre was introduced to me by his attending psychologist as a patient diagnosed with paranoid schizophrenia. He was diagnosed two years ago and comes to the ward weekly as an outpatient. I am happy that he is an outpatient, as, unlike Charlotte, he is more stable in his mood and is a more reliable informant where my data collection is concerned. Besides, Dre has provided me with so much understanding of what it is like to live in the world of a "paranoid schizophrenic". Dre shares his experiences with me and touches on the spiritual elements, which I am happy he addresses, as I often hear patients speak about the impact of the spiritual world on their illness. One of the major reasons for conducting the study which forms the basis of this book, is for me to get an understanding of how patients understand the role of the supernatural in mental illness. I often reflect on moments when I would ask patients what they believed was the cause of their illness and some would respond, "Is Obeah dem use pon mi" (Someone has used black magic against me).

Family members of some patients also share the belief in Obeah as they bring special oils to the ward to help remove the spirits from their loved ones.

Early in my clinical training I was taught not to entertain patients' ideas of being the victims of witchcraft, neither was I to allow them to practise the rituals on the ward. This meant that if family members brought oils into the ward I should inform them that this was not allowed. Whenever these oils were withheld from patients, they would become angry, and were adamant about obtaining their special oils. In our group therapy sessions, when given the opportunity to discuss their experience of the ward and the changes they would like to make, patients would raise the issue of their unfair treatment, which would include the withholding of their oils. It appeared that these dissatisfied patients depended on their traditional cures.

I realized from my interactions with each participant that every individual carries with them a storied life (Rosenwald and Ochberg 1992). A story assumes a Storyteller and an Audience; it is an intersubjective experience.

MY JOURNEY

> I am human and let nothing human be alien to me.
> —Irvin D. Yalom, *The Gift of Therapy* (2002, 21)

I was fascinated by the talk of Obeah, spirits and demon possession by patients on the psychiatric ward, and though I had heard of these experiences on numerous occasions, I was not allowed to entertain any discussion of the supernatural world with them. But based on the frequency with which they mentioned this, I was convinced that they had a different perception of their illness from that of their doctors. My feeling was that there were two sets of patients: one set believed that their illness was caused by spirits and would therefore seek the help of the traditional practitioner (Obeahman or woman, healer, herbalist); the other set believed that their illness was due to biological causes and would seek the help of the Western practitioner. I wanted to understand how the patients' worldview of their illness led them to seek the particular treatment, that is, Western biomedical or traditional.

As my training progressed, I continued to hear stories of the supernatural and I became even more convinced that they were important to the patients' perspective of their mental illness. The taboo against discussing patients' stories about spirits caused the stories themselves to retreat into the background. I resigned myself to a routine of entering the ward, performing my ward rounds and moving on. Despite the training to ensure that I only collected the necessary clinical information, I could not help but overhear patients explaining their varied illnesses as supernatural in origin.

I really wanted to know how prevalent the belief in supernatural causes was among the patients. The only way I could fully understand their belief in the supernatural was to study it. I had previously completed my master's paper examining this phenomenon despite being met with resistance from some members of staff in the academy. The concerns expressed were that this phenomenon was not measurable; that it was not a part of my training; and that studying it had implications for my designation as a clinical psychologist. Although I valued these opinions, I decided nevertheless to seek others who would support me on this journey (into the world of spirits). One of my supervisors told me of a medical anthropologist who had worked in this area and who was willing to help. We worked on my methodology and I insisted on using quantitative measures as a means of assessing patients' belief in the supernatural world.

My quantitative journey into the world of spirits had begun. Still, I felt disappointed in myself on completion of the master's in clinical psychology. On the one hand, I wondered how I would be viewed by others in the field, and on the other, I felt that I could have done more with the data so as to give more details on the patients' experiences. At the time, my own insecurities about how I appeared to others as a young professional were more important than my passion for the study. I therefore made the decision to do something more "scientific" for my doctorate, and for almost a year I parted ways with my interest in patients' experiences of the supernatural. However, the stories kept coming back to me and I had a longing to return to my main interest. Other classmates, aware of my interest in the patients' stories, would consistently tell me of the patients who were willing to share, and would encourage me to examine the topic once more. I was confused as to what to do, as I was almost a full academic year into my new topic. After deep reflection I made the decision that I would rather spend more time on something I was passionate about than on being concerned with my professional image. I decided to return to my "mad stories": "Mad stories are evocative and metaphoric. They are full of symbols, but we think that those symbols are used in very personal, even idiosyncratic ways. We consider them as incoherent and incomprehensible. They are not 'rational' and do not represent any 'normal' logic. They do not fit into categories. They escape every classification, save that of 'psychotic stories' or 'mad stories'. They are matters out of place" (Van Dongen 2003, 207).

COUNTING SPIRITS

I began my journey of understanding patients' stories by using a quantitative approach which I felt would have allowed me to note the trends and give clarity to the patients' experiences. I could unearth what it is like for the psychiatric patients to have a different worldview other than that of their practitioner, and what it means to be treated with an approach that may not be in keeping with their worldview. I had the opportunity to test my hypothesis that patients who believed that their illness was supernatural in origin were likely to seek help from the traditional practitioner. I was also interested in understanding the Western practitioners' perception of the patients' use of traditional oils and potions. My preliminary analysis of the data showed me that in quantifying these experiences I was only counting spirits. Other than the trends I noted – that patients who perceived their illness to be supernatural in origin were likely to seek traditional medicine – this quantitative data did not give enough details on the patients' experiences. To get at those details required that I use a qualitative methods approach. One of the approaches of qualitative methods that allowed me to document the meaning that the patients make of their experiences is a hermeneutic or interpretive phenomenological approach (Larkin and Thompson 2012). Cohen, Khan and Steeves (2000, 50) argue that in hermeneutic phenomenology, the participants should not be seen as "variables, but as people who offer a picture of what it is like to be themselves as they make sense of an important experience".

This approach takes into account not just the person and the meaning that they make of their experiences, but also the person in the context. Cohen, Khan and Steeves's (2000, 74) suggestion of the hermeneutic circle seems to provide a way forward, as an approach to how I could measure my participants' stories: "Using the hermeneutic circle as a means of interpreting

Variables		
		➤ Meaning
Year 1	Year 2	Qualitative
Quantitative study Trends, Variables, Frequency (N = 60)	Reflection on process	Phenomenology of 6 patients. Rich thick data.

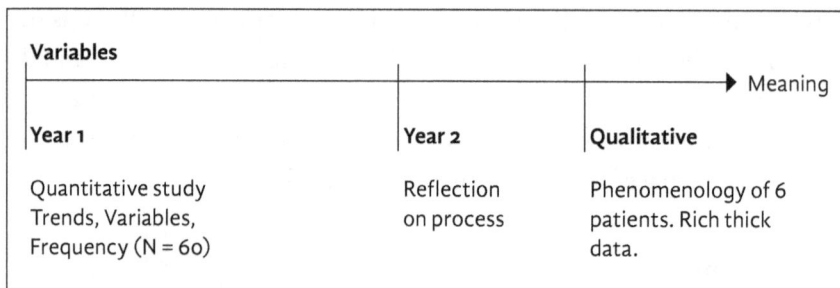

Figure 1. A timeline of my research journey

data means that the smallest statements must be understood in terms of the largest cultural contexts. It also means that the entire context in between must be taken into consideration; the person, the family and the community must be considered." I recognized that for me this was a transition where I moved from understanding the trends that existed in the quantitative data to a deeper meaning-making of the patients. This journey from quantitative to qualitative is outlined in figure 1.

THE RESEARCHER'S STANCE

The mixed-methods approach is not uncommon for health service research. Both quantitative and qualitative methods have been shown to complement each other, and together they both lead to a more comprehensive understanding (O'Cathain, Murphy and Nicholl 2007). In fact, in doing more research on developing and expanding the quantitative findings by using the phenomenological approach, I discovered the terminology that has been used for this type of combination: a mixed-methods phenomenological approach. This approach has not been formally conceptualized but is believed to have several advantages (Mayoh and Onwuegbuzie 2015). The main advantages are that the quantitative method and hermeneutic phenomenology are both philosophically similar and compatible, which makes it easier to combine the two methods, thereby adding rigour in order to understand a complex phenomenon. Further, the findings from the quantitative phase can help to identify the most relevant phenomenological experience to be explored. Lastly, a combination of the two approaches is justifiable as they each allow for the triangulation of the equivalent quantitative and phenomenological data and therefore increase the trustworthiness and validity of the study (Mayoh and Onwuegbuzie 2015; Patton 2001).

The usefulness of combining a phenomenological approach with quantitative methods can be illustrated through triangulation, complementarity, development, initiation and expansion (Greene, Caracelli and Graham 1989). Qualitative and quantitative methods can be mutually corroborative, making it difficult to contest their findings. Further, the results from the qualitative method can be used to help to enhance, illustrate and clarify the results of the quantitative method (complementarity). They both allow the examination of any contradictions, gain new insights and reconstruct questions (development/initiation). Finally, having collected the quantitative data, I can use the qualitative method for further explanation of the quantitative findings to therefore extend the depth of inquiry (expansion).

In applying the quantitative method, I am able to obtain information that relates solely to the area of interest. Quantitative data allow for a brief statistical method of analysis to capture a wide range of experiences of the participants in order for me to formulate an impression of the general trends that exist among this study population. However, it does not lend itself to detailed descriptions of the experiences of the participants, which are crucial to this study. While the quantitative research method is an effective method for data collection, it has limitations in capturing the discourse and realities of the participants as these relate to their experiences and the meanings that they give to their experiences. The qualitative segment of this research brings a more complete understanding to the experiences of the participants by lending description and meaning to the statistical associations found in the quantitative data.

My qualitative journey into phenomenology had begun. My main goal, having observed the trends from the quantitative data, was to reflect on the gaps that existed and to gain deeper understanding of this particular person-phenomenon. A more in-depth relationship with my six participants could give deeper meaning to the experiences I had already uncovered in the quantitative findings. According to Wojnar and Swanson (2007), phenomenological research is used to answer questions of meaning. It is most useful when used to understand an experience in the way that those who are having it understand it. I could not just assume what the patients' experiences were, as "only patients can reveal the meanings they create" (Cohen, Khan and Steeves 2000, 4). At the time I had not identified the salient theme – that at the heart of what participants wanted was an opportunity to tell me their stories and for me to share in these stories.

Yalom came to mind as I was thinking through the problem and the advice he gave to young therapists. Yalom (2002, 10) had taken a quote from Rilke and expanded on it. He stated, "Have patience with everything unresolved and try to love the questions themselves. Try to love the questioners as well." I began to give myself some time to think, but the more I thought the more I became frustrated in my desire for resolution.

Later that night, I was having a conversation with a friend who wanted to know the essence of what I was doing. More specifically, my friend wanted to know if my goal was to prove Western medicine was insufficiently thorough in addressing these patients' concerns and to highlight traditional medicine as being the practical solution. I remembered I responded by stating that my point was not to prove which was right from wrong, but that I simply had the need to understand the participants' perspective as it relates to their experiences of this phenomenon. I tried to further explain by posing two scenarios: "Let's say that you told me about a particular incident and your views on it; what preferred response would you like me to give? Would you like me to simply agree or disagree with your point of view? Or would you prefer if I displayed understanding of your experiences?" He took a moment to think about my question and then answered, "I think I would like to know that you understood. I don't want you to simply agree or disagree with me. That would mean that not only are you not hearing me, but you are dismissing what I have said."

This conversation became crucial in my understanding of what was to be done in my research. It was not that participants needed an elaborate presentation of what they had experienced; more importantly, they simply wanted to be heard and understood. In order to understand their perspective, I would have to start by first hearing their voices. I acknowledged my ignorance and cautiously embraced the experiences of the patients. When I opened the door of my mind, these voices came at full speed like the winds of a hurricane, lashing fiercely and occupying all the space in a way that was long overdue. The voices of Ariana, Charlotte and Dre were louder than ever.

The point that needs to be reiterated is that I am not saying that the patient's approach is right, neither am I saying that Western medicine is right. What I am trying to do is to highlight that these experiences need to be understood through the patient who is experiencing them. I decided that the participants and I would be fellow travellers. I was saying to each participant, "Take my hand and let us go on this personal journey. Help me to understand how you feel; help me to eliminate the blind spot that I have carried with me for so long." I felt the need to respond empathetically, to engage in conversation with each individual. The words that they expressed to me in the interviews are still alive, waiting to be understood and acknowledged. In essence, the specific phenomenological approach that I was using is hermeneutic phenomenology, which studies how people interpret their lives and make meaning of their experiences (Cohen, Khan and Steeves 2000).

The key questions guiding my research into the hermeneutic phenomenology of mental illness are first, "How do psychiatric patients conceptualize their own mental illnesses and what do they believe to be the origins?" and second, "Are Western practitioners open to patients' use of traditional medicine?"

CHAPTER 2

The Patients' and Practitioners' Worldviews

MY CURIOSITY ABOUT THE PATIENTS' PERCEPTIONS AND HOW their providers receive them was largely influenced by my recognition and acknowledgement of the grumblings that existed among the patients on the psychiatric ward. As clinicians, we are taught that we need not have the same beliefs as our patients, but we do have a duty to acknowledge them. Our ability to do so forms the very foundation for a good treatment relationship with our patients. It is therefore essential that we dedicate all our energies to truly listening and being attentive to the stories our patients bring to us. In essence, we should be open to seeing their worlds through their own lenses, which means putting aside our own personal opinions so as to truly attend to their stories. Nin (1961, 124) cautions us to recognize that "we don't see things as they are, we see things as we are". Therefore, we have to be mindful that in considering the perspectives of others, we as clinicians also have to account for the biases we may have based on our own worldviews.

Each individual's worldview is powerfully influenced by their own beliefs and personal ideology. The term "worldview" is derived from the German *Weltanschauung*, which means a view on the world, "used to describe one's total outlook on life, society and its institutions" (Wolman 1973, 406).

Although seen as an important construct in psychology, the idea of a worldview does not belong to any single comprehensive model or theory (Koltko-Rivera 2004). Researchers such as Koltko-Rivera (2004) and Leontiev (2007) have made attempts to create a theoretical framework to address the concept.

As a starting point for my own work I used Leontiev's (2007) theoretical approach to worldview, which encompasses the person's picture of the world – a general understanding of human beings, society, and the world, as it exists and functions. He describes worldview as an individuated construct, which consists of four structures. These structures include beliefs that the individual may share or may keep to himself, and standards for the world along with the need for consistency that confirms these deep-seated beliefs.

Worldview is shaped by a myriad of factors, of which history plays a significant role. In order to fully appreciate the worldviews shared in this book, I draw focus to the unpacking of historical events that layer Jamaican people's worldviews. Although no longer a colony of Britain since 1962, Jamaica still maintains the strong influence of Western dominance and the downplay of African retentions, albeit the majority of its population is of African descent. Researchers have found that this ongoing Western dominance may be linked to the colonial past and have developed an explanation called the colonial origins hypothesis (Acemoglu, Johnson and Robinson 2001). According to this assumption, there are two categories of colonialism; each category is defined by European settlement or the lack thereof. At the extreme end are the colonies where Europeans were unable to settle in, due to their low survival rates. These colonies, namely India and those in Africa and in the Caribbean, when compared to the other colonies where the Europeans had settled, had very different colonial states and institutions which continue to persist and form the foundation of the current institutions of these countries (Acemoglu, Johnson and Robinson 2001).

India and the African and Caribbean colonies were deemed as "extractive states" of Britain as they were subjected to harsh economic conditions; any economic gains derived from these countries were sent to Britain (Acemoglu, Johnson and Robinson 2001). The Caribbean at the time was seen as a profitable region as it had booming plantations and was well supported by labour from the enslavement and the forced migration of Africans. Despite the economic vessel that the Anglo-Caribbean was proven to be, none of the sums of money generated was invested back into countries like Jamaica. Countless studies have documented the ruthless actions taken by the British towards Africans in ensuring their physical and mental captivity to guarantee their continued labour. Despite being ripped from their homes and the attempts made by the British to eradicate their identities, Africans held strongly to their retentions.

Africans brought with them strong beliefs about health and wellbeing which were accompanied by traditional practices. In accordance with the African belief system, good health is considered to be holistic and the social environment plays an essential role. In order to achieve health and wellbeing, Africans incorporate medicines and rituals from traditional medicine (Cocks and Møller 2002). Traditional medicine existed long before Western medicine and is based on religious theories of illness and shamanistic magic ritual (Edwards 1986). Africans have relied on the use of indigenous remedies to ward off evil spirits and achieve personal wellbeing. Africans have employed various measures in order to achieve protection for themselves and family members, especially their infants, as infants were considered to be particularly vulnerable to harm from evil spirits. For protection they would wear certain ornaments such as protective necklaces (Pisani 1988, as cited in Cocks and Møller 2002). Another belief that Africans have is to maintain good balanced social relations by keeping one's dignity "avoiding envy and jealousy, limiting the effects of bad luck and giving support to the sick" (Cocks and Møller 2002, 387). When a person becomes ill it is often felt to be as a result of supernatural powers or witchcraft.

There are several reasons why the supernatural is believed to cause illnesses, one being that there are jealous relatives who use witchcraft to cause harm to the ones of whom they are envious. The persons who are more likely to be targeted by harmful spells are those who are seen as more successful, very intelligent and are high functioning (Cocks and Møller 2002). Another explanation for the supernatural being the cause of illness, is where the ancestors have been angered because their families do not engage in the appropriate rituals or offer thanksgiving, so the ancestors may in turn withdraw their protection, making their loved ones more susceptible to being harmed by spirits. These afflictions can occur through the grave, where the spirit of the dead possesses the individual, causing the illness to occur (Cocks and Møller 2002). The method of treatment is to find out who has caused the problem, whether a family member or ancestors (Mzimkulu and Simbayi 2006).

The African belief in ill-fortune is that illnesses do not just occur; there have to be reasons why and attempts to discover the contributing factors are either made through self-diagnosis and self-medication or through the help of a traditional healer (Cocks and Møller 2002). The methods of the traditional healer are not fully known to others, as it is believed that secrecy ensures that the treatment will work (van den Geest 1997). Traditional healers are guided by the ancestors to diagnose and treat individuals. Beliefs about health and well-being can cause anxiety for individuals. This results in the Africans relying on the traditional practitioner's concoctions and remedies to cope. Herbal remedies, brand medicines and synthetic fats are examples of substances used for the protection from evil, to bring good luck and fortune and therefore serve as reassurance for one's psychological wellbeing (Cocks and Møller 2002). Treatment may also involve cleansing of the individual as well as of family members and getting rid of spirits from the home through rituals such as singing and dancing (Mzimkulu and Simbayi 2006). The healer may also use cleansing methods by focusing on specific areas of the body such as the head and the stomach, or on the whole body and may use laxative herbs, steaming in herbs, vomiting through the nose and mouth or inhaling smoke through the nostrils to help the patient to relax. Treatment may also come in the form of a bath full of water with a mixture of herbs. Drinking and eating can accompany these rituals and are seen as forms of thanksgiving (Mzimkulu and Simbayi 2006).

Another form of treatment that the traditional healers offer is counselling of the entire family against the evil spirits and the encouragement of family members to perform certain rituals which include singing and dancing at the home of the patient to get rid of the evil spirits. This would be followed by slaughtering a white goat for the patient's ancestors and drinking traditional beer (Mzimkulu and Simbayi 2006).

The African worldviews on health and well-being are deeply held beliefs and practices which were brought to the Caribbean during slavery but were not permitted by the colonialists and were therefore practised in secrecy

(Pyne-Timothy 2002). Throughout the era of slavery, in territories such as Cuba, Haiti and Jamaica, African traditional religion was accused of being the source of rebellion for slaves. It was believed that once the slaves engaged in their religious beliefs and practices, this gave them a sense of power and control which would inspire them to rebel. Colonialists' intentions, therefore, were to ensure the successful enslavement of the mentality of the slaves, by enforcing a sense of powerlessness, insecurity and division (Pyne-Timothy 2002).

Naturally, the colonialists discriminated against African religion by labelling their retentions as "witchcraft", "superstition", "devil worship", "evil" and "folklore" (Pyne-Timothy 2002, 135). These stigmas are still deeply embedded within the social systems of the Caribbean and has resulted in the ongoing subjugation from imperialism to keep the African religious beliefs hidden. Despite these attempts, it is a known fact that African retentions, including rituals and beliefs, are deeply embedded in the psyche and consciousness of African people where their expressions can be seen in all spheres of life, including the works of writers and artistes (Pyne-Timothy 2002).

The failure to acknowledge African retentions continues to be even more pronounced in Jamaica, especially given the institutionalization of Euro-Western biomedical sciences. Western biomedical sciences are deemed as the more superior, modern scientific approach to health care and are the sole authority with regard to treatment. The principles of biomedical sciences are in stark contrast to those of traditional medicine. They originated in Europe and are rooted in the natural sciences model, based purely on empirical findings (Edwards 1986). The differences highlighted when biomedical sciences are compared to traditional medicine are that they do not have a religious component, they focus on the biological origins of illness, the professionals are detached, they use curative forms of treatment and the public is informed of their methods (van den Geest 1997). These Western scientific beliefs and practices have been known to dominate both Western and non-Western institutions. The Western scientific method of treatment has been hierarchically positioned as being the most prestigious and has marginalized African traditional approaches (Waldron 2010).

Therefore, the current dichotomy that exists between Western and African worldviews seems to be linked to historical events of the past. The past

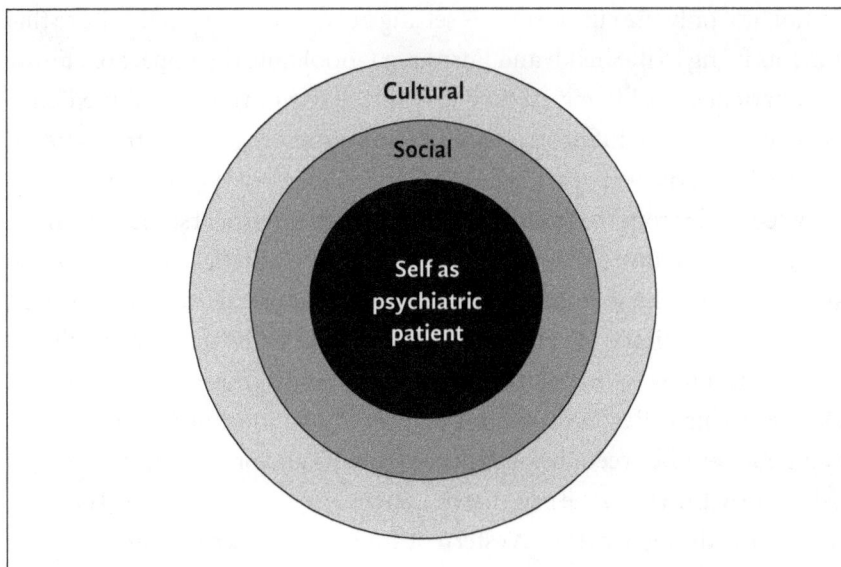

Figure 2. Patient's lifeworld

events as they pertain to Western dominance and the subjugation of African retention, continue to have long lasting effects on the present. One of the mechanisms that can explain the "historical persistence" of the relationship between Western and African retention is culture (Nunn 2012, s108). Nunn (2012) defines culture as decision-making heuristics which can be found in values, beliefs or social norms. Culture is the medium through which history is expressed and becomes more evident. Therefore, the beliefs, values and customs brought by the Europeans during colonialism continue to be apparent in the daily practices of the institutions of countries that have been classified as being at the extreme end of the colonial origins hypothesis. Taking into account Nunn's (2012) views on culture as well as Acemoglu, Johnson and Robinson's (2001) colonial origins hypothesis, the formal institutions in Jamaica such as health care, the education system and governance have been influenced by the British worldviews. It is therefore implied that should these institutions be faced with an approach other than their own, for example African retentions, they would react with discriminatory behaviours similar to those of colonial times.

My study takes place within the psychiatric context. This takes into consideration not only the culture of this setting but also the personal culture that patients bring to it. Sheikh and Furnham (2000) note the impact of culture on a patient's worldview, particularly in the use of traditional medicine. They reveal that an influential factor in understanding psychiatric patients' mental distress is their cultural health belief. Therefore, when patients specifically seek help from the traditional practitioner, it is understood within the context of the culture that the patient carries with them. Weiss (1997) also attests to this as he states that cultural beliefs and practices affect nearly all aspects of psychiatry. He places special emphasis on how our own cultural beliefs affect how we as practitioners assess and diagnose mental illnesses. Our beliefs also affect help-seeking behaviour and the mutual expectations of interactions between the psychiatric patients and practitioners. Cultural beliefs lie within both the psychiatric patient and the practitioner. The practitioner's training, whether Western or traditional, has a culture of its own (Engebretson 1994).

Differences between patient and practitioner cultures can and do affect the treatment outcome. Beaubrun (1966) notes that the Caribbean doctor, usually one from the middle class or social elite, usually schooled in the Western mode of medical practice, is typically unaware of his patient's beliefs and value systems. To further reiterate this point, Weaver (2003) states that young, intelligent people are drawn from the various cultures to undergo intense education and training in the Western biomedical sciences. After training, these health workers return to their respective cultures to practise their skills (Weaver 2003, 44).

Caribbean practitioners may encounter yet another difficulty obtaining and understanding a patient's clinical history as the patient may utilize lay terms or cultural idioms in presenting his problem (Beaubrun 1966). The literature, though sparse, indicates some common Jamaican folk medicine terms used by patients to express their spiritual and physical illnesses, which include "eyes dark", "bad feeling", "get out of self", "act ignorant", and "take it on the brain" (Wedenoja 1983, 240). Although this may strongly impact on the interaction between patients and Jamaican practitioners, it is noted more often with foreign practitioners who frequently diagnose personality disorders in patients whose behaviours go against their own norms (Hickling 1975).

Wittkower (1970) further suggests that West Indians display a form of cultural paranoia, which makes it difficult to distinguish paranoid symptoms from paranoid beliefs. Jamaicans when presented in England as psychiatric patients usually exhibit paranoia, which is sometimes based on the belief that their illness is caused by witchcraft (Kiev 1963). These cultural expressions are often labelled religious delusions and hallucinations in psychiatry, as they resemble the symptoms that are present in schizophrenic and manic patients. When patients experience symptoms such as withdrawal and noisy, aggressive behaviours, they frequently believe that the causes are demon-possession or sorcery, and usually seek treatment from the traditional healers (Beaubrun 1966). We see, therefore, that culture here refers not only to the larger context of national or regional culture but also the culture of the individual practitioner and patient.

This study examines the worldview of psychiatric patients in light of the conceptual model (figure 2). At the heart of the model is the concept of the self as a psychiatric patient. This may include a set of beliefs, values and notions of what constitutes normal or abnormal behaviour as well as a perception of the world. Outside of that lies the social context, which includes friends, family members, the community and public observable behaviours. The social lies within the cultural context and takes into consideration the role of psychiatry, the practitioner's and the patient's roles, traditional practices and spiritual/religious beliefs. All of this is embedded in the larger context of Afro-Caribbean history and practices, which include 150 years of pre-missionary, pan-African syncretic cults. This conceptualization of the individual takes into account not only the individual's worldview but also the individual within the larger context of their lifeworld.

PATIENT PERCEPTION

The Psychiatric Setting

The term "psychiatric patient" can only be understood within the context of the setting where both a psychiatrist and a patient exist. For this reason, Goffman's (1959) theory of the total institution is important as he looked at the psychiatric hospital and saw a closed system – a "total institution". This theory describes how the individual moves from being a person with their own self-concepts to occupying the "role and life-style" of a psychiatric patient. Goffman explains the culture of the psychiatric context where the nurses, psychiatrists, psychologists and other psychiatric patients shape the individual's self-view.

In the psychiatric setting, the lives of psychiatric patients are governed by a set of rules that demand that individuals conform to the role of being mentally ill. Upon entering this total institution, they may not initially see themselves as psychiatrically sick and in need of treatment. However, they may identify with being eccentric, possibly having difficulty getting along with other people or fitting into the norms of social life. As the social process unfolds, Goffman believes that eventually the psychiatric system manages to convince the reluctant individuals that indeed they are ill and in need of treatment.

This process begins with the development of the case history. This is purposely constructed to demonstrate that the patient belongs in the mental hospital, regardless of whether or not the patient believes this to be true. Goffman states that the process of convincing a person that he is mentally ill first begins with the alliance of three essential actors such as the complainant, the mediator, and the next-in-relation. The first actor, the complainant, notes that the "patient-to-be" has disrupted the norms and culture of everyday living and social expectations. The second actor, the mediator, represents an authoritative figure of the wider community. Their job is to recognize when there is any "trouble", especially as it relates to disturbance in inter-personal relationships. Examples of the second actor may be a policeman/woman, social worker, teacher or clerk. The third and final actor is the next-in-relation. This individual, which could be a family member or close friend, knows the patient-to-be very well. The first actor in noting the deviance in the behaviour of the patient-to-be, convinces the second actor. Together, the first and second convince the third actor. All three actors eventually become convinced that the patient-to-be is mentally ill and impose their belief on the "more than eccentric" individual.

In the total institution, otherwise known as the psychiatric hospital, the process of becoming the psychiatric patient begins to unfold. The health-care professionals (psychiatrists, clinical psychologists, psychiatric nurses, social workers) will interview individuals such as the complainant and the mediator who will attest to the changes noted in the patient-to-be that do not align with their typical behaviour or with what is expected of them based on societal standards. Next, the health-care team will make an assessment as to whether or not the individual falls within the realm of "patient".

The health-care professional then takes these "factual" behavioural reports from the patient's past and summarizes this information to fit into a coherent narrative. In this narrative, the individual will clearly appear to be mentally ill. Goffman notes that such a case history is not likely to attend to the times when the individual displayed "normal" behaviour in the light of difficult times. It is skewed towards a psychiatric interpretation. The case notes justify the placement of the person in the mental hospital. They attain a profound legitimacy that almost no one, especially the patient themself, can challenge.

HONOURING THE VOICES

The description given by Goffman introduces us to the complainant's, mediator's, next-in-relation's and the health-care professional's account of what is taking place with the patient-to-be. At no time are we introduced to the person experiencing the difficulty and their conceptualization of this difficulty. We have heard how the actors in this psychiatric setting will present their stories and the key actor – the patient – goes unacknowledged. According to Goffman, what is presented is the case study which has limited our understanding of what the individual/patient experiences.

To understand what the individual is experiencing, as clinicians we have to start by acknowledging what it means to be mentally ill and how the "ill" self is positioned in the body and the social world (Skott 2001). In addition to obscuring one's sense of self, the experience of illness is taken to the medical setting where the voice of the patient becomes lost as they are exposed to "impersonal or dehumanizing medical discourse" (McClean 2003, 486). In applying this "dehumanizing medical discourse", we miss out on the opportunity of interacting with and supporting the full experience of that part of our patient that is experiencing the illness and in dire need of our help.

Goffman's description makes it evident that the experience of being ill is framed in objective and depersonalizing terms such as disease, thereby removing the subjective experience of the illness from the individual. A psychiatric diagnosis seems to limit the individual's construction of their stories. Unlike physical illness that insinuates a temporary malfunction of the body, mental illness seems to give the notion that the individual is "fundamentally flawed" (Sakalys 2003, 137). For example, an individual who experiences a physical illness such as cancer is not labelled based on their illness. The individuals neither refer to themselves, nor are they referred to as "canceric". On the other hand, an individual with mental illness is labelled by the mental illness they experience, which then becomes a part of their identity. The individual who is experiencing schizophrenia is now known as "the schizophrenic". I take the position that it is imperative to acknowledge the unique subjective experiences of the individual and their mental illness. It is the interaction with the individual that becomes of utmost importance, acknowledging the subjective experience (Adame and Hornstein 2006). Understanding the patient's lifeworld cannot be reduced to measurable variables designed to prove or disprove a psychiatric diagnosis. Rather, the emphasis should be on understanding and interpreting "unrestricted personal accounts of particular experiences" (Murray 1997, 10; Bochner 2001).

In light of this, the traditional clinical dialogue will become transformed and the practitioners will no longer guide the patient's account of the illness in the frame of a diagnosis. Instead they lend an empathetic ear to the patient, thereby making meaning from the phenomena as experienced by the patient. Such an approach provides patients with an opportunity to be heard and gives greater value to their perspective (Sakalys 2003).

NARRATIVES IN THE PSYCHIATRIC SETTING: MAD STORIES

An important part of people's lives is narrative, and in medicine there is no exception. In order for these narratives to be useful in patient care, the stories that are told by the patients must be listened to, heard and validated by the healing professional (Gold 2007). On a daily basis, patients present their narratives to family members and health-care professionals. These stories provide insight into and knowledge of the patients' experience and act as a way of bonding practitioner and patient, a way of caring, healing and supporting individuals who have been diagnosed with psychiatric disorders (Gold 2007). Understanding the impact of the psychiatric disorder is crucial and physicians are invited to reconnect with the stories of their patients so as to transform the health-care system into a healing system.

In a psychiatric setting, practitioners and nurses generally ignore those stories that contain details of what they perceive to be hallucinations or delusions. These stories are viewed as "mad stories" that are "incoherent and incomprehensible" (Van Dongen 2003, 207). They do not fit into any category and do not represent anything that is "normal" or "rational". Psychiatric stories, although consisting of a wealth of information, are mainly subjected to one interpretation – the practitioner's – which seems to be the most powerful interpretation in the psychiatric setting (Van Dongen 2003).

Mad stories are viewed as symbolic and may lend themselves to many interpretations. German psychiatrist, Karl Jaspers for instance, indicates that although people with schizophrenia are diverse, they seem to display commonality in being "strange", "enigmatic", "alien" and "bizarre". Jaspers further suggests that these symptoms displayed by patients lie beyond the realm of human meaning and do not easily lend themselves to interpretation. Put simply by Jaspers, these stories are "ununderstandable" (as cited in Barrett 1998, 469). In the psychiatric setting, the stories of the schizophrenic escape every classification, except that which places them into the category of being schizophrenic, psychotic, or out of reality. The cause of schizophrenia is largely attributed to a brain disease and, therefore, practitioners focus less on the meanings of the stories that the patients present, and more on the refinement of diagnoses (Van Dongen 2003).

"Psychiatry transforms and reinterprets mad stories into 'medical stories'" (Van Dongen 2003, 210). The majority of scientific research done on schizophrenia ignores the meaning that the illness has in the lives of the individuals. The explanation given of the disease does not come close to explaining what the individual experiences. However, by telling these stories, patients become subject to the control of psychiatry and their expressions are not entertained, but rather are subjected to therapeutic and biomedical interventions. For instance, when patients present a complaint in a psychiatric setting, their narratives are reported to the practitioner and examined, to determine whether or not the patients have insight. The traditional unidimensional view of insight is "the correct attitude to morbid change in oneself and the realization that the illness is mental" (Lewis 1934, 114).

However, Amador et al. (1991, 114) argue for a multidimensional definition of insight. According to the multidimensional perspective, insight should have at least four dimensions – awareness of mental illness, ability to relabel psychotic experience as abnormal, self-awareness and the seeking of medical treatment. The approach to insight, as used by Western biomedical sciences has been criticized, the major flaw being that the term "insight" is a Western concept which only becomes effective if the person is of a Western biomedical perspective. Mental illnesses are classified as medical diseases, and a failure on the part of the patient to acknowledge this medical diagnosis is viewed as lack of insight. It is for these reasons that Saravanan et al. (2005) argue that insight should not be limited to one perspective as is the case in Western biomedicine, but rather should take into account the culture of the individual. Unfortunately, with the Western biomedical approach, other cultural explanations are often discounted or ignored. This is so even in societies like Jamaica where tension exists between traditional non-Western cultural beliefs and Western beliefs.

THE JAMAICAN PSYCHIATRIC SETTING

Patients who have been consistently admitted to Jamaican psychiatric hospitals over a period of time soon learn how to escape the psychiatric diagnoses and subsequent hospitalization by deciding when and how (to some extent) to present their psychotic stories. It has been noted that over time the stories told by psychiatric patients eventually lose their meaning, as, during the diagnostic process and interaction with health-care professionals the stories become contained and controlled, reflecting a rehearsed script (Van Dongen 2003). The mentally ill patient who would initially freely express the narrative of their illness, over time becomes the patient searching for psychiatrically acceptable details while hiding what they now see as unacceptable narratives.

Many aspects of an illness can only be learned from the individual who has experienced the illness. "The narratives of those who have recovered from psychosis come from voices that are often not heard. Like chronic pain, psychosis is often a silent, inner, and invisible experience that leaves observers guessing" (Gold 2007, 1272). Being natural storytellers, we construct stories that not only reflect our experiences but also ones that reflect our identity and the impact of culture in our lives. When we reflect on events that have transpired in the past, we remake and reconstruct those events to match what is occurring in the present. This process is one that is culturally shaped (Wang and Brockmeier 2002).

Culture, according to Kleinman (1980), can have an impact on the different ways in which we understand the body and the self. He invites us to understand that in the psychiatric setting there is a Western culture that proclaims Western medicine as technical, evidence-based and value free. Further exploration of this is given by Kuper (1999) who states that culture consists not only of the individual's knowledge, beliefs and attitudes, but also of the larger components of rules, relationships and practices maintained by social institutions and systems of power. When we as researchers examine culture, we tend to perceive it as though it is external to us and the environment in which we live. The challenge lies in understanding the external environment and in how that which is external is internalized.

To understand this phenomenon, we would therefore have to uncover the psyche of the individual. This is done through storytelling, where the stories are not just about us, but takes into account our thoughts about others (Kirmayer 2006). Narratives are not just words on paper, they are a reflection of self – our earliest connections, our impressions of the world, our passion as well as our silent moments. They reflect our stories – the ones we tell ourselves and others; they contain our thoughts, reflections and our imaginations. It is necessary then that narratives also be understood in terms of the social context, the audience to which it is directed and the interviewer (Kirmayer 2006). As researchers, we determine meanings based on the participants' stories, taking into consideration the larger social context such as the audience to which they are directed and the interviewer, noting Goffman's Impression Management which points out that individuals will want to maintain a certain image when telling their stories (Murray 1997).

The discourse in the narratives is important, as here we are able to capture the interaction that takes place in terms of how individuals develop their own self-narrative and how these narratives are influenced by their interaction with others as well as the wider society. From the interactional perspective, self-narratives may be influenced by the institutional norms of status and power. "Culture then appears as a set of institutional settings, formal and informal practices, explicit and tacit rules, ways of making sense and presenting one's experience in forms that will influence others" (Kirmayer 2006, 133). Culture needs to be understood at the individual level as these beliefs and understandings may vary depending on the social system. This system consists of different individuals who each have a unique view, each wanting to share their own "version of reality to dominate or take hold". Kirmayer (ibid.) indicates that when faced with situations like these we need to pay special attention to "the specific dynamics of each actor's story".

What we document when patients and doctors meet does not come close to reflecting the experiences of the patient. The language itself is also called into question, as what the patient says is framed by the context and the medical, social, and cultural factors that also inform the way in which the story is told. It has been argued that the discourse between patients and practitioners has been insufficiently studied (Skott 2001). The differences between patient and practitioners have been noted and practitioners have tried to bridge the gap by using narrative communication to bring further understanding to the experiences of the patient. It is through the study of narratives that Goode and Harrison (2000) suggest that we learn about culture and the construction of illness. Additionally, narratives act as a healing device where individuals create a balance between their bodies, identity and the world (Skott 2001).

As Caribbean researchers and practitioners, we have the unique opportunity to bond with our patients as we too share these historical and cultural perspectives. Though we may vary in the extent to which we embrace the Western and or African retentions, as Caribbean people we are very much aware of our history and culture. Therefore, when our patients bring their narratives, it should be understood that they are also bringing several parts of themselves inclusive of the historical and cultural selves. These parts of the patients need to be acknowledged in order to establish and maintain a trusting relationship. In preparation to receive these narratives, practitioners should also bring our cultural and historical awareness to the fore.

WITCHCRAFT, SPIRIT POSSESSION AND OTHER CAUSES OF MENTAL ILLNESS

British (Western) biomedical practitioners have frequently noted the discrepancies between their attribution of mental illness and that of the patients in their practice. They have frequently encountered psychiatric patients who are immigrants from Asia, Africa and the Caribbean claiming to have been bewitched or that someone had used Obeah against them. Although statements such as bewitchment or Obeah are culturally accepted in non-Western societies, in British society statements such as these might lead to a diagnosis of a paranoid disorder, which will result in the individual being placed on antipsychotic medication (Dein 1997).

Another cause identified by patients that seems to conflict with the Western practitioners' ideologies of mental disorders is spirit possession. Spirit possession occurs when a spirit or ancestor takes over the mind and the body of the individual, resulting in the possessed individual sometimes being in a trance-like state and acting out of character. In Africa and Asia, individuals freely admit to being possessed and having spirits speak to or act through them. In Western society on the other hand, admitting to this might lead to a diagnosis of schizophrenia. Administering medication to such a patient who believes that his problems lie in some paranormal or supernatural occurrence might not ensure compliance. The patient may feel the medication cannot address the problem and may disagree with the diagnosis (Dein 1997).

Jorm (2000) has noted the differences that exist between developing and developed countries with regard to their ideas of mental illness and the types of treatment that one would seek. In developed countries, it has been reported that visiting the psychologist and psychiatrist is more helpful in treating schizophrenia, yet less likely to be effective when compared to consulting general practitioners for the treatment of depression. These cultural beliefs in developing countries seem to be different. Patients in developing countries appear to seek traditional medicine as a part of their treatment regime not only because they believe that their illness is as a result of supernatural forces but also because they believe in the effectiveness of traditional treatments. The patients' perception of the causes of mental disorders is relevant as it will impact on their help-seeking behaviours and response to treatment. For instance, in Ethiopia, traditional treatments such as witchcraft, holy water and herbalists are preferred over medical help (Jorm 2000), while in Malaysia, the belief that one's mental illness is caused by supernatural forces resulted in greater use of traditional healers and less compliance with the medication provided by Western biomedical sciences (Razali, Khan and Hasanah 1996). A similar pattern was also found in South Africa where psychiatric patients who believed that their illness was due to supernatural forces were more likely to seek spiritual and herbal healing for the treatment of their ill health (Sharif, Ogunbanjo and Malete 2003).

Several studies have compared traditional healing centres with other non-traditional healing centres such as psychiatric hospitals in other parts of Africa (Peltzer and Machleidt 1992; Erinosho 1976). They found that the traditional centres had lower readmission rates but longer periods of admission, and better after-care continuity and social integration. This is an indication of the efficacy of traditional medicine, and there is empirical evidence of traditional and faith healers playing an integral role in health care in South Africa. There is also evidence of patients there and in other countries in Africa seeking the help of the traditional healer as their first choice in treatment for their ill health (Peltzer 2000). In a survey carried out on hospital patients and staff by Mabunda (1999, as cited in Peltzer 2001), participants revealed that a number of diseases could best be prevented or cured by traditional healing such as witchcraft and ancestor-related interventions.

The belief in the spiritual and supernatural as the cause for one's illness is prevalent in countries in Africa and the Caribbean. There is consistent evidence in the studies conducted in parts of Africa that illustrates patients' use and belief in the efficacy of traditional medicine as compared to Western medicine. This is understandable as traditional medicine seems to be more closely aligned with the Africans' cultural beliefs on health and well-being.

PATIENT PERCEPTION OF TRADITIONAL MEDICINE

Integrating Traditional and Western Medicine in Treating Mental Illness

The empirical evidence indicates that traditional medicine has been sought as one of the first treatment options by Africans, and some indicate that it is effective. Despite this, it has not been given much prestige and has been frowned upon and marginalized on the basis that it represents mystical and magical religious belief (Peltzer 2001). Efforts on the part of Western biomedical practitioners to convince psychiatric patients that their mental illness is not attributable to supernatural forces have been futile, resulting in the conclusion that this belief system is deep-seated and difficult, if not impossible, to eliminate (Muller and Steyn 1999). This is not to say that patients who believe in the supernatural completely ignore the Western scientific approach. Bruce (2002) points out that these patients may accept scientific westernized medicine but retain traditional concepts in order to give meaning to their experiences.

It has often been argued that patients also incorporate both traditional medicine and Western biomedicine into their treatment, in order to achieve holistic treatment of the physical, mental, and spiritual. Traditional medicine is needed for the spiritual, whereas Western biomedicine is needed for the physical (Rowe and Allen 2004). The spiritual dimension forms an integral part of the individual's worldview. That conditions the person's interpretation, comprehension and reaction to life experiences and explains why individuals will turn to their religious faith when ill (Rowe and Allen 2004).

Patient Outcome and Objective Outcomes: Two Perspectives on Effective Treatment

The World Health Organization (WHO) defines health as "a state of physical, mental and social well-being, not merely the absence of disease or infirmity". This definition has been in existence since 1946 and has not changed since (WHO 1946). It is important to note that the WHO's definition does not take into account the spiritual aspect of the individual and may therefore influence the medical models in their perception of what treatment entails. In fact, one of the major flaws of Western biomedical science is that generally it does not address the spiritual aspect of the individual nor does it provide for the treatment of mental illnesses in a holistic manner. Further, the objective outcomes of the effectiveness of Western biomedicine are not necessarily related to patient-based reports. A good medical outcome does not necessarily equate to good patient outcome. Looking at the outcomes from both perspectives can assess the difference between the patient's views and the objective medical perception. Medical treatment can only result in partial or temporary amelioration of symptoms (Ellison and Levin 1998).

Western biomedical science can eliminate symptoms that are testable and visible by that standard, but it is felt to be ineffective in circumstances where patients attribute illness to factors derived from supernatural entities such as spirits or chance (fate/luck) (Ellison and Levin 1998).

TRADITIONAL AND WESTERN MEDICINE IN JAMAICA

In some societies that have a strong African heritage, psychiatric patients simultaneously seek treatment from the traditional healers as well as from Western practitioners (Peltzer 2001). Jamaicans also follow this pattern in treating their ill health (Wedenoja 1983). Whereas in some parts of Africa the use of traditional medicine is openly acknowledged and accepted as part of the management of psychiatric illnesses, in Jamaica, traditional medicine is practised in secrecy and is frowned upon by those who are unaware of the nature of its practice. This lack of knowledge is further exacerbated because certain practices are illegal. The Obeah Act of 2013 states that anyone who uses or pretends to use supernatural powers or knowledge is liable to imprisonment with or without hard labour. This law extends to other individuals who seek help from the Obeah man or woman and individuals assisting in anyway (Ministry of Justice, Jamaica 2013). Coupled with traditional medicine being seen as socially unacceptable, this results in a paucity of research in this area. The term "Obeah" is currently used in a loose and vague manner to include practices under the sphere of traditional health and traditional medicine (Weaver 2003). Despite the stigma and legal repercussions attributed to its use, the majority of psychiatric patients admitted to using traditional medicine in the treatment of their ill health (James 2012).

Religion is one of the key features in traditional medicine, and Jamaicans are known for being extremely religious. For the first 150 years of slavery in Jamaica there were no Christian missionaries on the island, therefore, a set of pan-tribal religious institutions developed. It was around the 1800s that Methodist, Baptist, and Presbyterian missionaries began to arrive and this resulted in the development of Afro-Protestant syncretic cults (Wedenoja

1983). Subsequently, the American evangelical and Pentecostal sects became strong movements (Wedenoja 1983) in which the rituals usually involved faith healing by group prayer and the laying on of hands. Syncretic revival or pocomania cults took on a form of healing which involved herbalism, otherwise known as balm. In 1968 Marriot (as cited in Wedenoja 1983) completed a survey which indicated that at the time 32 per cent of the psychiatric patients believed in balm healing, and 8 per cent went to a balmist. These figures are however a gross underestimation and quite dated.

Balmists

The balmists (diviners) are usually older women, called "mother" or "maddah" in Jamaica, who receive a visionary calling to practice. They usually have an office and a church near their homes and mix African herbalism and divination with Christian beliefs. They give advice to patients on interpersonal problems, on nutrition, and prescribe mainly "bush" (herbs, roots and barks) for treatment. Some prescribe special candles and prayers. Due to the belief that the illness is of supernatural origin using "bush" alone without rituals and faith is considered ineffective (Wedenoja 1983). Rural peasant patients, in particular, have been reported to hold the belief that mental illness can be caused by Obeah or some spirits. Royes (1962) suggests that it is helpful to have some knowledge of these folk beliefs.

Long (1973, as cited in Wedenoja 1983) examined reasons that patients chose to visit the balmist for their health problems and found that not only did they feel that it would be effective, regardless of cost and time, but that the patients and the balmists were of the same status and subculture and had better rapport and communication. Patients feel that they can adequately explain their problems to the traditional healer who will give them enough time in which to do so.

Another reason for choosing the balmist was based on the patients' classification of their illness. They distinguish between psychogenic or interpersonal and organic illnesses. They go to a balmist for alleviation of the interpersonal illnesses but to the medical practitioner for the organic (Long 1973, as cited in Wedenoja 1983). Balmists were generally considered to be more effective in treating psychological illnesses and to give superior psychosocial counselling, whereas physicians were viewed as more effective in treating organic illnesses (Long 1973, as cited in Wedenoja 1983).

Wedenoja (1978) reports that the Pentecostal sects and revival cults were felt to offer more psychological support than balm. Researchers such as Ellison and Levin (1998) note that there is a positive association between religious involvement and health outcomes which results from the role of religious communities in providing social support. Wedenoja (1978) also finds similar trends in Jamaica; he goes on to explain this as being due to this group providing members with emotional and material support. This practice often offers individuals the opportunity for catharsis and emotional and aesthetic expression, particularly in possession trance experiences.

Patient Perception: Diagnoses/Labels

Medical practitioners are often concerned with the psychiatric patient's response to hospitalization. Often patients insist that nothing is wrong with them and that they do not belong in the hospital and refuse to comply with treatment. Psychiatric patients' inability to recognize that they suffer from severe mental illness and are in need of psychiatric care is generally perceived by the practitioner as a lack of insight as a result of the cognitive deficit that accompanies mental illness (Sayre 2000). The patient's interpretation of their own situation is seen by the practitioner as unreliable, a symptom of the psychosis. This is further exacerbated by the practitioner's approach to helping these patients become functionally stable so as to return to the community to operate in their normal capacity.

The hospitalization procedures lead patients to believe that they are helped neither to understand what has taken place, nor to improve their ability to take care of their lives more effectively. Hatfield and Lefley (1993) are of the opinion that the process of diagnosis and hospitalization only confirms the patients' sense of failure. Individuals who have suffered from severe mental disorders such as schizophrenia and bipolar disorders reveal that one of the most painful and dehumanizing aspects of living with their diagnosis is the loss of their personal identity in being labelled with a mental illness (Schyett and McCarthy 2006).

Practitioner Perspective: Formal Procedure

One of the major differences between the traditional and the Western practitioner is that one is known as a healer and the other a curer. The traditional practitioner, usually referred to as a healer, offers holistic treatment through spiritual means. The ailments are therefore addressed spiritually. "Curing", on the other hand, is a Western biomedical term which refers to helping to reduce or get rid of physical symptoms or disease (Engebretson 1994). In order to understand the distinction between both approaches, the cultural and historical elements of each need to be understood.

Prior to the seventeenth century, Western practitioners incorporated principles from traditional medicine. The practitioner viewed the individual not in terms of being separate mind and body, but that the body, mind and spirit were unitary forces. The medical practitioner was therefore considered to be both a medical and spiritual leader. Western biomedicine was released from the patronage of the church in the seventeenth century. This shift away from the mind-body unity came at a time when philosophers such as Descartes were arguing that the mind and the body were separate entities, and paved the way for Western biomedical practitioners to conduct autopsies and understand the human body, without being concerned about disturbing the soul (Engebretson 1994). Western biomedicine throughout the age of reason continued to break ties with religion as the scientific revolution stressed rationality, reductionist science and a sceptical secularism. The scientific method placed more emphasis on the mechanical workings of the body and continued to enforce demarcations between the mind, body and spirit (Engebretson 1994).

TRAINING OF WESTERN PRACTITIONERS

Western biomedical practitioners are trained in a formal institution where teaching is firmly rooted in a scientific paradigm in which the explanation of the causes of disease is through a biomedical model (Bruce 2002). The Western biomedical approach is sanctioned by practices of licensure, certification and accreditation (Council on Scientific Affairs 1999) and practitioners use technology to diagnose and treat mental illnesses. Treatment includes drugs, medical interventions and psychotherapy (Bruce 2002).

The discipline of psychiatry is a Western scientific mode of treatment that was specifically developed to address mental illness. Psychiatry was established in the nineteenth century during the emergence and consolidation of industrial capitalism in the West. This mode of treatment was designed to address abnormal and bizarre behaviour which did not comply with the demands of the new social and economic order. Abnormal behaviours were classified based on what a person said and how they behaved. This process, known as diagnosis, places the disorder within an existing system or group of disorders (Sarason and Sarason 1999). For the psychiatrist, mental disorder is defined by a variety of concepts such as "distress, dysfunction, dyscontrol, disadvantage, disability, inflexibility, irrationality, syndromal pattern, etiology and statistical deviation" (American Psychiatric Association 2000, xxx).

Wilhelm Griesinger (Sarason and Sarason 1999) believed that mental illnesses were as a result of the direct or indirect influence of disturbances in the brain; as a result, he developed the slogan "Mental diseases are brain diseases". The research led psychiatrists to conclude that mental illness is due to a chemical imbalance within the brain. Therefore, disorders such as schizophrenia are believed to be due largely to the fact that in the brain, the chemical dopamine is overactive, whereas depression is due to the depletion of the chemical amines, such as serotonin. In an effort to correct the chemical imbalance, certain drugs were produced to reduce the overactivity of dopamine in the case of schizophrenia and to produce more serotonin when addressing depression (Sarason and Sarason 1999). In the 1950s and 1960s the physiological causes of mental disorders were further highlighted as pharmacological companies began to produce an array of drugs to address specific mental illnesses such as schizophrenia, depression and anxiety (Siebert 2000).

An important criticism that psychiatry has and continues to endure is that although it has created drugs to address mental illness, these drugs have never cured it. Even the most modern drugs are said to be no more effective in actually bringing a cure to mental illness, yet what is noted is that they bring numerous side effects (Siebert, 2000).

OPENNESS TO TRADITIONAL MEDICINE

Westberg (as cited in Griffith 1983) has advocated a holistic care concept, in which he has proposed the collaboration between Western biomedically trained physicians and religious leaders, in the diagnosis and treatment of patients. He seeks to legitimize the role of the church in the healing process by purporting that healing is a natural ministry of the church. Healing in the church could help individuals to move towards a more mature faith in God and this in turn could impact on bodily reactions, which would allow individuals to enjoy greater health. The holistic approach to clinic care would encompass the spiritual, mental and corporal components of the human being, based on the belief that one becomes more vulnerable to disease when alienated from God through sin. As such, curative intervention would be most successful when the individual moves towards reconciliation with God (Griffith 1983).

While not disputing the fact that there exists the use of traditional medicine among their patients, Western practitioners tend to be strong advocates of the scientific method. Additionally, it is also argued that Western biomedical practitioners cannot accept a liberalized health-care system as this reduces their dominance and produces competition (Weaver 2003).

According to Hayes and Watrall (2000, 1), practitioners of Western medicine in believing that their approach was the most effective approach to health, regard traditional medicine as "weird and outlandish, clearly a product of ignorance and superstition . . . unscientific and virtually untestable". Their approach to the diagnosis of ill health, on the other hand, was thought to be more effective, as they viewed their approach as "rational and scientific".

To be more specific, it has also been argued that Western practitioners lack understanding when patients attribute their illnesses to anything other than that which is scientific. This lack of understanding, researchers reveal, is due largely to the fact that Western practitioners tend to have the misconception that rational reasoning can change the deeply held beliefs and values of their patients towards their illness. Therefore, they may think that if they present rational arguments then the patient will comply. But refusing to acknowledge the patients' approach to health and forcing them to follow the Western approach can have catastrophic results. Elaine and John

Cunning, in reporting the ultimate demise of one mental health programme commented, "It was evident that we have been trying to change ideas that were deeply held and that the more we tried to dislodge them the more tightly people held to them and angrier they become at us for trying to take them away" (Simon and Pardes 1985, 272).

From as early as 1966, Beaubrun in the Caribbean stated, "It would be a mistake to underestimate the importance and influence of these religio-magic practitioners. They have a head start over the orthodox middle-class practitioner of medicine in that their ideas of the aetiology of mental illness are shared by their patients and they are much better grounded in the culture than he" (54).

Beaubrun (1966) also warned that although patients did seek balms it was illegal to do so. Noting that balm is a practice lacking in prestige, he advised that psychiatrists should not promote collaboration with traditional healers as happens in Nigeria. Western biomedical physicians often reject requests from their patients to incorporate spiritual healing in their treatment because the scientific has been legitimized and has "proven objective" advances in the reduction of morbidity, disease progression or hospital readmission (Miller and Thoresen 2003, 24).

One approach to patient care is the Common-Sense Model which gives a description and comparison of patients' and practitioners' perception of the causes and treatment of mental illness.

COMMON-SENSE MODEL

The Common-Sense Model, developed by Leventhal et al. (1991, 1992, 2001, as cited in Insel, Meek and Leventhal 2005), is an ideal one for this study, as it predicts that illness representations will differ between practitioners and patients, based on different experiences and education. In providing a theoretical framework for understanding why and how they differ, Leventhal, Brissette and Leventhal (2003) posit that illness representations can be examined through five lenses – *identity, timelines, cause(s), consequences* and *control*. I will use this model to depict the differences from first, the patients', and then the practitioners' perspectives.

Psychiatric Patients' Conceptualization

The first lens, *identity* refers to the labels of the concepts and associated symptoms. It has been established that patients' explanatory models can provide insight into lay beliefs about their illnesses. This may include the personal, historical and social meaning of the illness and what they expect will happen as a result, as well as how and when they would expect the practitioner to intervene (Okello and Neema 2007). Patients may perceive their illness as one that naturally occurs or "just happens". This would include illnesses present from birth, such as mental retardation and epilepsy, as well as common illnesses ranging from colds to chickenpox. These types of illnesses are seen as common in all societies and can be dealt with by the Western practitioner.

There are other illnesses which are felt to be specific to Africans and are felt to be only understandable within African concepts of illness, and, as such, can only be recognized and treated by traditional healers (Crawford and Lipsedge 2004). Within this paradigm, mental illnesses and psychological distress may be conceptualized differently in the traditional context. Illnesses such as depression are felt to be caused by spirits, are felt to debilitate the individual's functional ability, and are considered to be more serious than chronic medical illnesses. The distinction as to the type of illness that exists is imperative as this has implications for help-seeking behaviour (Okello and Neema 2007). Remnants from African cultures on health perception still remain a rich part of Caribbean people's conceptualization of their illnesses (Wedenoja, 1983).

The next lens to be considered is *timeline,* which refers to the time of occurrence or duration of the onset of the illness, measured by the experientially felt time. The timeline of the illness will indicate its type, and how it should be treated. If the individual is born with the illness then it is interpreted as natural; however, if the individual suddenly becomes ill and was not known to have had this illness from birth, then it is regarded as unnatural.

For instance, the "throwing illness", which is felt to occur when the victim is asleep and dreaming and may cause mental illness, has symptoms which seem similar to those of a patient diagnosed with schizophrenia. According to the belief, in order for this to occur, a person who wishes another ill prepares special medicine and rituals and transmits this illness to the victim without physical contact. This results in the victim having a serious or even fatal illness, which can only be rectified if the perpetrator is identified by a skilled traditional practitioner (Crawford and Lipsedge 2004). Therefore, the nature of the symptoms and access to an expert traditional practitioner will give the patient an idea of the duration of the illness.

Also important is the perception of *cause.* Among Africans, sorcery is commonly perceived as the cause of mental illness. Sorcery can be used by anyone who bears a grudge against another. Eskin (1989) also found that in Third World countries mental disorders were usually attributed to super-natural/mystical beliefs.

Next are *consequences* which refer to the imagined or felt experiences of the individual. An example of this is the "stepping over" illness. This is where the wrongdoer may sprinkle medicine in an area where they suspect the victim is likely to walk. Once the victim walks in that area the victim may fall ill with several symptoms such as "loss of appetite, loss of strength, joint pains, headaches, abdominal pain and loss of enthusiasm". They may also experience "insomnia, hypersomnia, bad dreams, memory loss, poor concentration, trembling, dizziness and sweating" or may even become suicidal (Crawford and Lipsedge 2004, 134)

Finally, *control* refers to ideas of cure and control as opposed to experience with specific control agents. Patients experiencing these manifestations/spirits or mental illness will resort to the help of the traditional practitioners as they are the experts in the area of working with spirits. These illness representations are important as they guide the selection of procedures for preventing and controlling illness and establish criteria for evaluating their efficacy (Crawford and Lipsedge 2004).

Western Practitioners' Conceptualization and Treatment of Mental Disorders

Leventhal, Brissette and Leventhal's features apply in a far clearer way from the perspective of the Western practitioners. For *identity,* individuals are considered mentally ill if they present with any disturbances in behavioural or psychological functioning that are not culturally accepted, and that lead to psychological distress, behavioural disability, and/or impaired overall functioning (American Psychiatric Association 2000). This information is gathered through careful history taking, where the health-care professional interviews others who can attest to the changes mentioned above, and through a psychiatric evaluation conducted by the practitioner.

Regarding *timeline,* the practitioner will assess if there has been any psychosocial stressor, or change or event that has caused the symptoms to surface.

Several models may be used to explain the *causes* of the illness – the biological, psychological, sociocultural and the diathesis stress model, with the biological model being the main explanation in Western medicine. The models are defined as follows:

- Biological disorders are understood in terms of malfunctions in portions of the brain, imbalance in various neurotransmitters and genetic factors.
- The psychological model emphasizes psychological factors in the development of mental disorders. For instance, some psychologists believe that learning plays a key role in many mental disorders (e.g., learning phobias).
- The sociocultural model emphasizes external factors such as negative environments – poverty, homelessness, unemployment, inferior education and prejudice – as potential causes of some mental disorders.
- In the diathesis-stress model, mental disorders result from a predisposition for a given disorder (diathesis) and stressors in an individual's environment that tend to activate or stimulate the predisposition (Sarason and Sarason 1999).

Consequences are the psychological distress, behavioural disability, and/ or impaired overall functioning (American Psychiatric Association 2000). Finally, *control* results when, in an effort to correct the brain chemistry, certain drugs are used – to reduce the over-activity of dopamine in the case of the schizophrenic, and to produce more serotonin when addressing depression.

Western biomedical practitioners possess a body of information about the causes and consequences of mental disorders and detailed knowledge of treatment options and anticipated outcomes, which does not take into account the spiritual dimension (Insel, Meek and Leventhal 2005). The medical model postulates that patients' rejection of a psychiatric diagnosis is due to their lack of insight, which the practitioner concludes is indicative of the cognitive deficits consistent with their mental disorders. In this case, the patients' illness representations are not only rejected but treated as meaningless (Sayre 2000). The patients who have the subjective experience of their mental illness may feel that Western practitioners who are mere observers with different experiences and illness representations are unable to identify with their needs and are unable to help them manage their mental illnesses more effectively (Insel, Meek and Leventhal 2005).

THE CLIMATE OF PSYCHIATRY IN JAMAICA: THE INFLUENCE OF HISTORICAL AND SOCIAL EVENTS

Researchers have documented the psychological effects of slavery, colonialism and post-colonialism on the psyche of Caribbean people. These historical events do have an impact on the treatment and management of psychiatric patients (Hickling 2010). As Jamaica was a colony of Britain, the management of mental illness was dictated by its mother country. Therefore, similar to its mother country, Jamaica adopted a custodial approach, where the police could arrest and charge for lunacy. Jamaica also incorporated the inhumane treatment of the mentally ill, where persons were locked in asylums, beaten and chained. These approaches to mental health went through major transformations after Jamaica gained independence from Britain in 1962 (Hickling and Gibson 2012).

This transformation of psychiatric care took into account the social and cultural needs of the Jamaican people (Hickling and Gibson 2012), with the first monumental change being the transfer of the rights of patient management and treatment to medical doctors and nurses. Doctors were given the rights to detain and admit individuals involuntarily if they were considered a threat to themselves or others (Mental Health Act of 2013). Patients typically stayed an average of fourteen days in the psychiatric hospital, compared to Britain which had a longer admission stay (Hickling and Gibson 2012).

It is not surprising that the transformations that occurred within the medical system were as a result of continued advocacy of two Caribbean-born psychiatrists, who were trained under the Western biomedical system in England. Perhaps their desire to influence changes that were specific to the needs of the Caribbean people may also have been as a result of them sharing the historical and cultural legacies of the Caribbean people. Through their efforts, along with the University of the West Indies (Mona) and the Jamaican Ministry of Health, they were able to achieve deinstitutionalization and community mental health services (Hickling and Gibson 2012). Still, the Western biomedical approach remains the dominant approach to psychiatric care, with the main treatment apparatus being pharmacology, while the other approach offered by Western biomedicine is psychotherapy. These treatment modalities are administered by psychiatrists and clinical psychologists respectively. The goals of the psychiatrist and clinical psychologist are to diagnose and treat psychiatric patients, however, their administration of care differs.

A psychiatrist is a medical physician who has postgraduate training in treating mental illness. Psychiatrists are given the legal responsibilities in the commitment proceedings and in the supervision of mental hospitals. The psychiatrist's typical approach to treatment is to administer medication. A clinical psychologist, on the other hand, holds a graduate degree, typically a PhD or PsyD, and specializes in abnormal behaviour. Clinical psychologists are trained to diagnose and treat persons who are mentally ill, and their treatment approach is psychotherapy (or talk therapy). They are also trained to conduct research (Sarason and Sarason 1999).

The use of medication as the main treatment modality for the overwhelming numbers of patients may be the most viable option for Western biomedicine as psychiatrists have a heavy caseload with a ratio of 1:100,000 (psychiatrist to patient) treating over forty thousand patients per year (WHO 2009). Unfortunately, being the most viable option does not necessarily mean being the most effective, especially if there are limitations in addressing other key areas that are important to patients' needs and overall well-being. While this biomedical approach may address the biological aspects of the mental illness, it neglects the other aspects, including the psychological, social and spiritual. One study has shown that Jamaican psychiatric patients who also accessed traditional medicine in treating their illness were dissatisfied with their psychiatric care. These patients felt that Western biomedicine should also incorporate traditional medicine in their treatment regime (James 2012). The ideologies and expectations expressed by these Jamaican psychiatric patients seem to resonate with African cultural worldviews (Edwards 1986).

Fortunately, psychiatric care in Jamaica did eventually address the psychological needs of patients by introducing psychologists to administer psychotherapy (talk therapy) as well as to conduct psychological assessments. This offering, however, is difficult to access by most psychiatric patients, as psychologists in Jamaica are few in number. Perhaps the number of trained psychologists is a reflection of the development or introduction of psychology as a discipline in Jamaica. Unlike psychiatric training which was introduced in 1965 to medical doctors and nurses at the University of the West Indies, psychology was introduced thirty years later, and this was only at the undergraduate level (Hickling and Gibson 2012).

Psychology came on board as an undergraduate specialization in 1995 in Jamaica and Trinidad and Tobago, and in Barbados in 2000 (Ward and Hickling 2004). However, undergraduate level training is insufficient, with a minimum of a master's degree being required for qualification to work with psychiatric patients. The sections of psychology and psychiatry at the University of the West Indies (Mona) offered a joint master's and PhD programme in clinical psychology, where its first cohort of master's students graduated in 2003 (Ward and Hickling 2004; Hickling and Gibson 2012). Despite the return of overseas-trained native psychologists to the Caribbean, along with graduates from the clinical psychology master's programme (Hickling and Gibson 2012), the ratio of psychologist to psychiatric patients still remains low at 0.388 to 100,000 (WHO 2009). This is an indication of a void that needs to be filled. Even though the demand and publicization of psychology continue to be on the increase, most persons are unclear about the differences between a psychiatrist and a psychologist (Hickling and Gibson 2012). This is an indication that there is still a lot more to be done in educating professionals and lay persons alike.

In summary, the main treatment approach to mental illness that obtains in the Caribbean is the Western biomedical approach. While its main mode of treatment is pharmacology, it does offer to a lesser extent other psychological services such as psychotherapy. This service, however, is a scarce commodity. While the current offerings of psychiatric care aim to address the biological and psychological needs of its patients, it does not address the social or the spiritual. In countries with backgrounds and economic climates similar to

Jamaica's, the inclusion of traditional practitioners as part of its health-care practice is accepted and well sought after by patients and even encouraged by Western practitioners (Edwards 1986). Despite the evidence that Jamaican patients do include traditional medicine in their treatment (James 2012), it has not been welcomed by the Western biomedical model that currently exists in Jamaica. While the Western biomedical model may be effective at primarily the biological level, psychiatric patients have expressed a desire for more (James 2012).

Notwithstanding this, there is hope for further advances in Jamaican psychiatric care. Thus far, there has been the successful implementation of deinstitutionalization, community mental health systems and also therapeutic modalities which incorporate cultural elements such as sociodrama and psychohistoriography (Hickling 1989; Ward and Hickling 2004; Hickling and Gibson 2012). These, coupled with the ongoing research, will continue to inform practice. Research findings have indicated that there is still room for improvement, specifically as it relates to the quality of the day-to-day interactions that we have with our patients (James 2012). Improvement in taking the time to acknowledge patients' psychiatric experiences and taking more care in recognizing and validating what truly matters to our patients are essential. Further research incorporating quantitative and qualitative approaches may be needed to better understand and identify ways to address these needs.

CHAPTER 3

The Approach I Used to Hear My Participants

THE DATA USED TO ANCHOR THIS BOOK WERE gathered using both quantitative and qualitative approaches. Prior to data gathering, ethical approval was granted by the Mona Campus Research Ethics Committee of the University of the West Indies. All participants gave written consent and to maintain confidentiality, all identifying information was removed and not included in the study. Pseudonyms have been used for all six participants.

For the quantitative component, I used semi-structured interviews with the sixty psychiatric patients and thirty Western practitioners. My decision to include sixty psychiatric patients was to capture the wide range of their experiences in the Western biomedical setting, as well as to get their views on traditional medicine. My primary goal was to understand whether or not there were commonalities among these patients. In doing so, I wanted to know if these patients shared similar views on the treatment approaches. And finally, did the patients used in my sample conceptualize their illness in the same ways as their practitioners? Although my quest was to get at the patients' perspectives, I also had an interest in the Western practitioners, as their views on traditional medicine would allow me to get a more complete picture of the patients' experiences. Even though Western practitioners were trained using a scientific rubric, I was curious about their worldviews and if this reconciled with that of their patients', especially given that they too lived in a context where traditional approaches were often spoken of and were embedded in the culture.

After gathering this quantitative data, my next step was to have a deeper understanding by immersing myself in the qualitative findings. The six patients that I included in the qualitative section would shed more light on the discussions of the sixty patients. They allowed me to have a more in-depth understanding. The qualitative method allowed for "guided conversation" which enabled me to systematically look for and listen carefully to what was being conveyed by the participant "so as to hear the meaning" (Kvale 1996). In psychology, the subjective accounts of patients are essential to our field. This builds the foundation for the relationship that we have with our patients and also gives us insight as to how best to meet their needs.

My journey to acquire this information started at a psychiatric ward in an urban hospital setting as well as at an outpatient clinic at a hospital in a rural setting. The urban hospital is located in the capital city of Kingston in Jamaica and serves patients island-wide. The rural hospital serves the southeastern section of the island. My reasons for choosing these two locations were deliberate: the hospital located in the urban setting offered me a mixture of patients' views from all over the island; the hospital in the rural setting is located in one of the parishes that is strongly connected with traditional medicine. This parish has been associated with Obeah, traditional healers and herbalists. At the time, I was confident that the rural hospital would have afforded the opportunity for patients to share their traditional experiences with me, thus deepening my data further.

Prior to interviewing the patients, I had to ensure that they were psychologically able to answer the questions of the interview. The Western practitioners assisted me in identifying patients who were

- not actively psychotic – meaning their thoughts were coherent and logical. According to the practitioners, these patients did not exhibit signs of thought blocking, preoccupations or delusional thinking; their perceptions should lack hallucinations and should not be interacting with internal stimuli;

- verbally coherent; and
- able to attend sessions that ranged from thirty minutes to an hour and demonstrated an adequate attention span.

I conducted interviews with thirty males and thirty females, as I wanted to get balanced views from both genders. I had a wide cross-section of ages, ranging from seventeen to seventy-two with a mean age of thirty-five. Most of the patients in my study's sample were diagnosed with either schizophrenia, psychosis or an affective disorder.

My journey originally started with sixty psychiatric participants. Through a semi-structured interview I was able to gather information on their perceptions of their illness, the treatment they sought, as well as their evaluation of the treatment(s) they received. I also had the opportunity to meet with the practitioner participants. The mix of these different perspectives provided me with information on the Western practitioners' evaluation of the traditional approach and this compared to the Western approach. The data collected informed how I approached the qualitative analysis. Before examining the qualitative data, the information from the tape-recorded interviews had to be transcribed.

THE QUALITATIVE TRANSCRIBED

My data analysis process started with the transcription of the various stories that were recorded on tapes. The tapes were securely stored to ensure the privacy of those who shared their experiences with me. Fraser (2004) proposes that transcription of the tapes could be useful as they provided a more accurate record of the interview than memory alone, especially for those individuals who wanted to examine the data line by line. I spent some time on each interview, examining them repeatedly, gaining a *true essence* of the six participants' *worldviews*. I did not clean up the data, that is, I did not remove any information that may have appeared to be irrelevant. This allowed me to reflect over the number of pauses and moments of silence during each interview, as these emotional pointers created more meaning (Fraser 2004).

The transcription of the data was time-consuming but beneficial, as it brought me closer to the stories of the individuals. I realized the benefits of participants' recounting their experiences with mental health issues, which a qualitative approach allowed for. I wanted to learn more but questioned whether or not that would be possible, given that I had only two interviews for each participant, totalling one and a half hours at least. I began to feel discouraged, thinking that I had not captured as much as I could have. I also began to think of the ethical issues of spending more time with the participants and how that would affect their treatment outcome. I contemplated whether or not these stories would have changed had I conducted more interviews. I scoured the literature to see other researchers' assessment on the content of the narratives of psychiatric patients' stories, what they often refer to as mad stories.

Van Dongen (2003) reveals that "mad stories" as a whole tended to be consistent. He further reiterates that he followed psychiatric patients for many years, read their files, and it appeared that over the decades, though these stories were similar and never changed, they were not recognized as each individual's "subjective truth". I considered what I had documented, and I felt that what I had was the "subjective truth" and further, that in these narratives I had more "subjective truth" of the participants to uncover. Myers (2002, 325) describes the patient's construction of their illness as a "dynamic process in which threads of multiple narratives are combined and recombined to fashion a story that both forms and expresses the patient's experience". Although one narrative might be obvious and expressed verbally, there can be other narratives beneath the surface that are not in the patient's realm of consciousness but actually have an impact on what is being expressed. Young (Groleau, Young, and Kirmayer 2006) further supports this view by stating that individuals use multiple representational schemas and modes of reasoning to produce illness narratives that are complex and sometimes contradictory. The researchers' suggestion of multiple layers in narratives motivated me to re-examine the participants' stories with the intention of looking beyond the surface.

While I had in my possession these valuable narratives, I realized I had to spend time explaining how I arrived at the conclusions from the qualitative data. I learned that this approach has to be one where I am able to make clear the stories of the six participants, without any personal biases.

My intention was to ensure that their stories were heard and honoured. The theoretical approach that I used to analyse the qualitative data is hermeneutic phenomenology.

HERMENEUTIC PHENOMENOLOGY

Origins and Theoretical Premise

Phenomenology is considered an ideal research method as it interprets the experiences of an individual. The term was first proposed by Edmund Husserl who introduced the concept of "lived experience" (Mak and Elwyn 2003). According to Husserl, we gain meaning from our everyday lives; however, we take for granted our life meaning because we have not fully explored our "everydayness". Husserl believes that as researchers, we can get at the truth by exploring what we take for granted. He coins the studying of the everyday experiences through his examination of the subject-object concept. He argues that the subject-object is critical in understanding how researchers can get at the truth, whereby the individual is the subject, who tries to make sense of the environment, which is the object. In order to learn the truth, the individual has to examine the object, but this requires that they suspend their preconceived notions of the object through bracketing (Mak and Elwyn 2003).

Husserl's work was later significantly modified by his successors such as Heidegger, Kierkegaard, Sartre and Merleau-Ponty which created some diversity in the field of phenomenology (Wojnar and Swanson 2007). They created seven unique streams of phenomenology. Of the seven, the one most suitable for this study is hermeneutic phenomenology. The term "hermeneutic" comes from Hermes, the Greek god responsible for making messages clear, or for interpreting the messages between the gods (Thompson 1990, as cited in Lopez and Willis 2004). Hermeneutic, or interpretive phenomenology, focuses on interpreting the structures of an individual's experience. In a nutshell, the term hermeneutic is used to describe the interpretations of how a person understands their social worlds and how the researcher who is studying this person understands themselves in this context (Lopez and Willis 2004). The meanings behind one's life experiences are not always obvious to the participants but can be garnered from their own narratives. The primary use of the hermeneutic approach is to draw focus on the individuals' experiences rather than on what they are currently aware of, or what is consciously known (Solomon 1987).

For Heidegger, the social and the personal go hand-in-hand and, therefore, he rejects Husserl's use of the term "subject-object duality", since one cannot separate oneself from one's environment. In being-in-the-world or lifeworld, the individual brings with them a combination of their historical and traditional context, both of which have already influenced the individual's interactions (Mak and Elwyn 2003). Heidegger believes that the individual is influenced by the world in which they live and focuses on how we can use these preconceived ideas to understand the meaning of our own existence.

Believing that we are interpretive individuals, he expands on the definition of hermeneutics resulting in three different ideas. First is the concept of *dasein* which means being-in-the-world (Cohen, Khan and Steeves 2000). To be in the world, we have to take into consideration the individual in various contexts, such as the historical, social, political and cultural, which will impact on the meaning individuals give to their experiences and the choices they make. The second idea has to do with how we go about understanding our world as it is given to us, and third, understanding the meaning of being (Cohen, Khan and Steeves 2000).

Gadamer modified Heidegger's hermeneutic phenomenology by examining the use of preconception/pre-understanding before interpreting the findings. The term "pre-understanding" comes from Heidegger's being-in-the-world (*dasein*). According to Gadamer, one should use this pre-understanding not as a personal bias but as a pre-condition to the truth (Mak and Elwyn 2003). Pre-understanding is impacted upon by the person's past experiences (forehaving), perspective (foresight) and preconceived notions of what to expect in the interpretation (fore-conception). All three – forehaving, foresight and fore-conception – serve as the initial horizon of understanding. It is during the process of data analysis that the researcher's horizon interacts with the data (patient's transcript). The fusion of horizons results in new understanding. This process involves continuous "reflection, questioning and validation within the dialogue between the researcher and the text" called the hermeneutic circle (Mak and Elwyn 2003, 396).

We often conduct research on psychiatric patients, as if they exist only within the confines of their psychiatric diagnosis. We therefore take for granted the world in which they live and the influence this might have on them. The influence of the patients' outside world can become even more complex when they enter into a discourse with another individual who also carries and is influenced by a world of their own. Such is the case for patient-practitioner or patient-researcher interaction. Though these types of interactions may appear on the surface to be simplistic, they each contain multiple layers which can impact the meaning patients make of their experiences. That being said, the multiple layers of these engagements have to be taken into account if the researcher wishes to understand the lived experience of the psychiatric patients. Information garnered from these types of analyses can have a profound impact on informing health service research, especially in a region that is underserved and understudied, such as the Caribbean. The above-mentioned theoretical underpinnings of the hermeneutic approach guides this data analysis. The methodology entails preparatory steps as well as interpretive steps, all of which have been delineated in the following sections.

PREPARATORY STEP 1: CONSCIOUSNESS AS THE STARTING POINT

The process of examining my encounter with the participants and their stories, its nature and intensity, required that I resort to absolute aloneness, concentrating fully and intensely, examining what appeared before my consciousness. I examine what is in my memory, perception, judgement, and the feelings that I am experiencing. My effort is to ensure that I am actually in solitude where my conscious experiences allow me to channel my energy to attend only to the details of each participant's story as it appears to them and nothing else. The stories of the participants and the immediacy of the present direct my thinking. What is relevant is my perception, my own acts of consciousness, which at all times must remain as pointers to uncover knowledge, meaning and their *truth*.

My ultimate intention was to gain fuller understanding of each "mad story". The process is like rallying in a tennis game where my mind becomes the racket and the tennis balls the "mad stories". Each "mad story" enters my level of consciousness, resonates and then I send it back, with a different perspective. When I receive this information, I view it through a different lens; I examine each side of the ball using different angles of the sweet spot of racket. On one side of the racket is the clinical psychologist who has a peripheral view of the "patient" because of her training. On the other side of the racket, there is the individual who can understand and empathize with what it feels like to be silenced. This *silenced understanding* becomes the advocate for the unleashing of the "mad stories". Finally, there is the part of me that recognizes what it must feel like to be trapped in another world, similar to the participants' report of being trapped in "depression, negative energy, fire, devil, evil spirits and people being envious".

In this equation, one side of the ball (the ball representing the participant) sees and evaluates everyone's perspective of these "mad stories" – "family members, healers, psychiatrists, church members, nurses, etc.". There is the side that plays the role of the patient: "I do as I am told." Finally, there is the side that speaks of and is not afraid to share these experiences: "The doctors say it's hallucination, I say it's an encounter with the devil." Though I was able to use consciousness in order to locate the varying perspectives and the roles of the researcher and patients, there is still more that needs to be done before I can delve fully into the interpretation of the data. Taking into account Gadamer's instructions to become more aware of past experiences (forehaving), perspective (foresight) and preconceived notions of what to expect in the interpretation (fore-conception), I prepare myself to become more open and to fully delve into a deeper understanding of the patients' narratives.

PREPARATORY STEP 2: BRINGING AWARENESS TO THE DIALOGICAL EXCHANGE

In light of the position of the individual who has been diagnosed with a psychiatric illness, the conceptualization of the individual in the role of the patient neglects all the other facets of the individual, such as the patient, the person without the illness and the person who is trying to take control of their life. These different facets impact on any relationship that is being established. Put simply, when patients and practitioners engage in interviews, they each bring their individual feelings, fantasies and experiences to the therapeutic setting. These cognitive processes actively impact on the relationship that is being established, whether intended or otherwise. When we engage in an interaction, each person shapes this encounter (Ogden 1994). In hermeneutic phenomenology, it is very important that as a researcher and as a clinician, I am conscious of how my experiences are shaped by my participants' interactions as research subjects and vice versa. It is my intention to describe the "experience where consciousness exists, rather than study emotions or thoughts in the abstract" (Cohen, Khan, and Steeves 2000, 6).

Therefore, when analysing the patients' stories, we should pay special attention to our responses to the stories, taking into account our own narratives, our roles and our evaluation. It is important to acknowledge that these stories are interpreted by our own lenses. Our stories are shaped and reshaped based on the meanings that are attributed to those stories, based on our own cultural background. We therefore push "our stories against the stories of others . . . At the very least we are asking, if not insisting that others interpret their stories in light of ours" (Cottle 2002, 535). Ultimately, what we hope to gain is to be able to listen to the stories of others, but not without immediately responding to our own stories. To allow the process of listening to the stories to take place, we have to remove our own lenses and allow the words of others to enter us and see them for what they truly are (Cottle 2002). We therefore need to be aware of our own stories and the impact they may have on the nature of the relationship that we are establishing with our patients or research participants.

PREPARATORY STEP 3: THE VALUE IN IDENTIFYING OUR PRECONCEIVED NOTIONS

The intimate relationship that I have had with these participants' stories has been an interplay of ideas between the themes emerging from the data and my own personal and professional selves. To encounter the stories in a non-biased way, I have to start by first being aware of and confronting myself about who I am, and the factors that shape my own story – my own narrative, my own history. It is through my encounter with my participants' stories of them being the storyteller and me being the listener, that I have come to gain awareness of who I am in light of my experience with the other. "Without me, the Other can do nothing – it is utterly vulnerable and exposed" (Levina, quoted in Cohen 1986, 27–28, as cited in Cottle 2002). Each encounter with each individual has transformed my perspective. This stable image that I have tried to maintain so consistently is challenged and brought into question. Now I can see the different sides of me. In this process, I have the advantage of seeing my interaction with the data from multiple angles: from the lens of the researcher, a clinical psychologist, a Western practitioner, a Jamaican and a person with her own thoughts and feelings.

INTERPRETIVE STEP 1: UNDERSTANDING THE ROLE OF THE SOCIAL CONTEXT

I began to reflect on my personal journey as a clinical psychologist in training. In my seven years of training (BSc to PhD), I had learned how to truly listen to the stories of the clients. For me, it was more than listening with my ears (what is said and how it is said), it was giving honour to the non-verbal cues in order to gain the true experiences of the client. I began to ask myself the question "Have I truly been listening?" Here I was in awe with enthusiasm, being non-judgemental, encouraging participants to unveil their experiences, to tell their "mad stories". I must admit at first their reactions were ones of surprise when I asked them to share these stories. Many asked if I really wanted to hear or asked me not to share this information with the physicians so as to prevent their stories from "getting out". I assume that what caused them to share was a yearning to really tell their stories and my willingness and desire to listen.

Others were suspicious and queried whether I was a psychiatrist or a psychologist. Being a psychologist in this case had its advantages, based on the perceptions of the patients with whom I had interacted. These patients seemed more relaxed. Some told me that they had been looking for a psychologist to speak with for some time but had not found any. Others gave up their suspicion of my intentions and were ready to share their stories. Although I appreciated the time spent in their telling me these stories, I did not fully grasp what this meant to the participants. Once patients were admitted to the psychiatric ward, they lost control over their lives. This was further complicated by the fact that their stories, their lived experiences, were categorized as "culturally inappropriate" and not recognized to be "true" (Van Dongen 2003). Putting in context where and how the stories were shared, aided with my own understanding of the patients' lived experience and the ways in which the psychiatric institution impacted their engagement.

INTERPRETIVE STEP 2: THE PROCESS OF BEING-IN-THE[IR]-WORLD

When participants shared their stories with me, this was confirmation for the psychiatrist that they were not getting better and therefore risked being kept in the institution longer. I appreciated their willingness to take this chance with me. For me, as a fellow traveller in the world of their "mad stories", the telling and retelling allowed me to experience "being-in-the[ir]-world" through the use of "embodiment" (Merleau-Ponty and Smith 2002). Embodiment allowed me to identify with and better be able to understand some of the emotional experiences of the participants.

Being with the patients made me recognize and understand some of the emotions they felt. More profound was the fact that they were initially hesitant to share these emotions; however, upon building further rapport, there was more disclosure. I opened myself to this awareness and to being patient when they allowed me to see these emotions. I became grateful for these opportunities and I allowed these emotions to enter my consciousness. I began to see through their emotional exchanges what it had been like for them to not feel heard or to feel undervalued. Documenting these emotions and perceptions was essential, as I wanted to recognize the meaning that patients make of their experiences: frustration, anger, guilt, misunderstanding and emptiness. Having validated the patients' emotions and perceptions, it became easy for me to place myself in their position, to fully understand their silence within the confines of the psychiatric setting of not being able to share their "mad stories". Each patient construed their own meaning as it pertained to their experience. Understanding these unique experiences can be achieved through an idiographic approach.

INTERPRETIVE STEP 3: THE IDIOGRAPHIC APPROACH

For me, the hermeneutic approach calls for the researcher to make meaning of the *person-in-context*. My awareness was heightened when one participant in particular gave her personal accounts of her experiences of what it is like to be labelled with a psychiatric disorder. An idiographic approach therefore became necessary. This approach focuses on the individual as opposed to the general (Harper and Thompson 2012). I took note of Husserl's encouragement to become aware of the role of my history, culture and this context. In addition to my own social location, I also recognized what Heidegger and Merleau-Ponty highlight the fact that we are inseparable from the relationships we form with others and that our engagement with our world shapes our awareness. I noted that my initial response was that of the practitioner, matching the symptoms described by patients such as Charlotte to a psychiatric diagnosis. The psychiatric diagnosis is a starting point. In acknowledging that part of myself, my story, I came to see a different perspective. The paranoid schizophrenic who exhibits "Preoccupation with bizarre delusion(s) or frequent auditory hallucination(s)" (American Psychiatric Association 2000, 314) became an individual to me through repeated attempts at listening to her *voice*. The "static label" is no longer sufficient to describe this person who is more than her diagnosis. Charlotte's life does not exist on a diagnostic sheet; it contains broader aspects that are not overshadowed by her illness. I discovered features of her personality such as her tenacity in fighting for her right to be treated as an individual who is "spiritual, creative, different", and so on.

An idiographic approach to the narrative of each participant – Noel, Charlotte, Ariana, Dre, Fiona and Thomas – became necessary if I were to honour their unique experiences. Each patient makes meaning of the change that has occurred in their lives, irrespective of whether or not they have been given a psychiatric label; they make a decision as to how they will name this experience. The influences of the Western and or traditional approaches to their current challenges were also highlighted. In the participants' narratives they illuminated their family's and/or community's response to their condition. Though the idiographic approach is said to elucidate the "concrete, particular and the unique while maintaining the integrity of the person" (Eatough and Smith 2017, 10), its application in psychology claims to be limited, as there is an emphasis on making inferences to the general population (Allport 1940). Here hermeneutic phenomenology plays a critical role as it begins with a detailed analysis of the unique experiences of the individual which may also be shared by other individuals (Eatough and Smith 2017).

The hermeneutic approach also allows for the creativity of the researcher, where the research has diagrammatically outlined these experiences. The diagrammatical illustration can be impactful in understanding patients' perception of how their worldviews align with that of their practitioners'.

INTERPRETIVE STEP 4: THE CREATION OF CONCEPTUAL MAPS

I found that transposing the patients' information onto conceptual maps was useful to get a clear picture of their journey and how they resolved their treatment. I first synthesized the raw material into logical, meaningful categories, guided by the Common-Sense Model (Leventhal, Brissette and Leventhal 2003). I paid special attention to the participants' representation of their illnesses, the course of the illnesses and their expectations as to how they should be treated. I also examined participants' perception of the Western and traditional practitioners' diagnosis and treatment and the extent to which they agreed with the practitioners. It should be noted that all the patients received treatment in keeping with the Western biomedical approach and had shared their experiences and evaluations. These have been included in the conceptual map. When it comes to their perceptions of traditional medicine, I included the information that the patients shared about the actual visits to the traditional practitioner as well as any references made to the use of the spiritual/supernatural methods in helping them to cope with their mental illness.

While conceptual maps are useful, they can only be fully appreciated if one has gotten to know the six patients' stories and their unique journeys that led them to some form of resolution in coping with their mental illness. The conceptual maps were intentionally placed at the end of chapter 5 as the information before that helps in situating these findings.

INTERPRETIVE STEP 5: EXTRACTING THE MAJOR THEMES TO TRIANGULATE WITH THE QUANTITATIVE FINDINGS

Having heard the true voices of the patients and having unveiled the *layers of meaning* from the idiographic approach, I extracted the major themes (essences) that were recurrent throughout the data. I compared both tran-

scripts from the quantitative and the qualitative interviews of each participant for amplification of the themes that I found. I used the descriptions
and themes in each transcript to develop an exhaustive description of each
participant's experience of the phenomenon: this is *situated structural description* (Daniels 2005). After creating a *situated structural description* for each
participant, I compared them all with a view to identifying common or
unique themes that occurred among the participants (Daniels 2005).

In summary, I have delineated a step-by-step process that entails three
preparatory steps and five interpretive steps, which I used to analyse the data.
The strategies outlined will aid the reader's understanding of the conclusions
drawn and inferences made in chapters 5 and 6. Before illustrating these
findings, an introduction of the key participants becomes necessary, as an
important part of this work is to acknowledge the individual behind the story.

INTRODUCTION TO PARTICIPANTS

Noel

I meet Noel in my office, which is upstairs in the psychiatric ward at the urban
hospital. His psychologist informs me that he is waiting for me outside the
door. Noel knocks, pops his head in, and smiles when I acknowledge him. I
ask if he is ready for our interview and he answers in a pleasant receptive tone.
Noel is a Caucasian male from a middle-class socio-economic background
and resides in an urban area. He is approximately 5 feet 7 inches tall and
medium built. He has dark brown eyes, his hair is neatly cut, his face shaven,
and he is comfortably dressed in a blue t-shirt and jeans. His mannerisms
seem older than that of a nineteen-year-old. We walk to the interview room.
His familiarity with the premises means that he knows which room we are
going to use. He opens this door for me, waits until I sit and then he sits. He
moves his chair closer to mine and waits patiently for me to start my tape
recorder. I remind him about our last interview and that today I need him
to give me more time and detail. Noel informs me that he has taken the time
off from work so he could do this interview. I felt that time was no longer an
issue and I could truly listen to his story.

It seems as if it is very important to Noel that I understand his story. I would pass Noel in the waiting room where, as an outpatient, he was always on time for his weekly appointment with his psychologist. He had promised me the week before that he would meet with me for our follow-up interview. Noel has a keen interest in psychology and tells me that he has been doing some reading to understand more about his condition. Noel speaks in a gentle tone, taking time to express himself, while at the same time putting it in the context of my professional understanding. I can tell that he is trying hard to remember every detail of his past and how it has impacted on him. It is very important for me to take this journey with him and each time he stops to ensure that I am included or can see it from his perspective. He gives me a detailed description of his family situation highlighting both positive and negative aspects. Although his family consists of two religious denominations, he aligns himself with one denomination as their approach to religion brings him more comfort in his dilemma. Noel initially thought that he was demon-possessed when he first heard himself lashing out at God.

He currently takes comfort in the fact that he is diagnosed with paranoid schizophrenia rather than being demon-possessed. The thought of him being possessed by the devil is far worse for him than being labelled with a mental illness. Noel tells me of his experience of an enmeshed relationship with his mother due to his father's infidelity. She would take him along to spy on his father's girlfriend, which was an uncomfortable experience for him. Noel feels that his difficult childhood is as a result of both parents possibly suffering from mental illnesses themselves, and therefore making them unfit to be parents. Throughout our discussion, he at times discloses that he works in a community where he is in frequent contact with murderers. He shows me a different side of himself, where he explains to me that he can identify with these murderers because of their difficult childhoods. He tells me that some had witnessed their mothers being physically and sexually abused. He believes that because they were exposed to this atrocity, they became murderers and he equates this with being mentally ill. Noel relies on his religious faith and he believes that one day they will all be saved from their sickness and suffering. According to him, beneath every mentally ill person lies a gentle, kind soul.

Charlotte

Charlotte is a twenty-four-year-old attractive Caucasian female, from a middle-class socio-economic background and resides in an urban area. She is approximately 5 feet 2 inches in height and is slender built. Her hair is done up in a ponytail and she wears a loose white top with a pair of jeans. Her face is long and oval and she has flawless skin and light brown eyes. These eyes for the most part give the impression of scrutiny. She is very proper and controlled in her behaviour. She stands in an upright composed manner. Charlotte is aware of the state of the facility and tries not to come in contact with any germs. She carefully chooses where she sits, where she stands and to whom she speaks. She seems to be above average intelligence and is very articulate. When I first approached Charlotte on the ward, she became suspicious of my interest in her. After completing the first interview, she is excited at a second opportunity to share the details of her story to fully explain why she was admitted on the ward. For our second interview, she makes it a point of duty to inform the nurses and psychiatrists that I will be coming to see her and that we should not be disturbed. She displays an air of self-importance, one that is above others who are unable to see her traits. She is intrigued at the idea of me jotting down her words and tape-recording our conversation. On our way to the interview room, she fills me in on the patients' diagnoses and how they are doing with their treatment – if they are on too much or too little medication. For those on a higher dosage of medication, she tells me a little about their personality. Her knowledge of these patients and their diagnoses sets the stage for her own defence against her diagnosis of paranoid schizophrenia (James et al. 2013, 252).

It seems as if I am her student and she is the doctor giving me a tour of the facility and how it operates. I feel that she is rushing me to make sure that I keep up with her and that I take note of all she has been telling me. Charlotte seems completely removed from the facility. It is as if she is in no way a patient. She plays this role of doctor very well and I play mine as the student. I give her the power because it is important for me to learn her cause. Her physical and mental separation from the inpatient facility is indicative of her refusal to accept her diagnosis. We go into a room that is at the far end of the ward so as to get as far away as possible from the other patients' voices. Charlotte examines the room and seems to find a seat most suitable for her, the one by the window. She waits patiently, watching me while I set up the tape recorder. She inquires if the recorder is on, leans forward then asks me if there is a purpose for this interview. This is puzzling to me; I nevertheless answer her question. I tell her that it is for me to get a better understanding. She smiles, leans back in her chair and says that I can continue to ask her the questions.

In the middle of the interview, there is a knock on the door. I am about to get the door when Charlotte gets it. She opens it wide enough so I can see who it is. It's a nurse. Charlotte inquires why she is interrupting us. The nurse explains that she wants to give her her medication. Charlotte is annoyed at her and reminds her that she is in an interview and that she should not disturb us. She tells the nurse that she will get back to her, and closes the door. She feels pleased with herself. She walks back to her seat with her head held high and her chest upright. She exclaims, "The nerve! Continue!" I hesitate at first as I do not want to interfere with her treatment. I wait to see if the nurse is going to return. She does not; so I continue.

Charlotte is an intriguing individual. She admits to not being "traditional" but more of an artistic, creative person with a deeper understanding of this world. She is very intuitive and I begin to learn that she can connect with the world at a spiritual level. Her ability to tap into energy to create art makes her unique from other family members. She fights to make it known that her qualities are similar to other unique devout Catholics such as nuns and priests. Charlotte is confident throughout our interview. She demonstrates pride each time I am in awe and show interest in her story. I can see the gleam in her eyes which seems to state "Hah! And there they thought that I was a paranoid schizophrenic. Here is someone whom I have schooled, and who understands my uniqueness." Throughout our interview, she makes sure to inform me that her diagnosis is incorrect, and that she does not belong on the psychiatric ward. She finds evidence to prove to me that the label "paranoid schizophrenia" is the malicious intent of her mother and uncle who have teamed up against her in their effort to control her. Their task was aided by the psychiatrist who is not a spiritual man and has no knowledge of the spiritual world.

Ariana

Ariana is a forty-five-year-old mother of three from a middle-class socio-economic background and resides in an urban area. She is a nurse practitioner who is diagnosed with bipolar disorder with psychotic features. She is approximately 5 feet 9 inches tall, medium built, and of dark complexion. She is dressed in a t-shirt and a long skirt and seems unkempt. Her hair is unprocessed and loosely plaited, and her eyes are bright. She is a devout Sunday worshipper. Ariana appears to be the victim; a person who is unfairly treated by the Western biomedical system. She believes that certain members of staff are out to make her become "mad and walk the streets naked". She is also suspicious of them over-medicating her and stealing her money. Ariana is happy at the opportunity to share her story with me.

I meet her on the steps while she is speaking with one of the nurses. She interrupts their conversation by asking me if I am ready for her. Ariana is talkative and is happy for the interruption, otherwise she would have continued the conversation, and promises the nurse that she will. We go into the interview room and she sits upright in her chair and folds her hands. She nods her head, indicating to me that she is ready to answer the questions that I have for her. Ariana describes herself as a brilliant individual who has enemies, including her mother. The problems that she is currently experiencing can only be as a result of two factors, her hyperthyroidism as well as witchcraft that others have placed on her. She complies with her medication to keep the thyroid from acting up, but complains to me that medical staff sometimes tried to use her medication as a means of punishing her. She takes pride in the fact that she is a nurse, as she is able to note the dosage of medication she is receiving and modify if necessary.

During our interview she tries to befriend me so as to get information to her psychiatrist because she wants early release so as to accompany her son to the US embassy for his visa. Ariana appears to be testing me, at first presenting different sides of her to see how I feel about ghosts and evil spirits. When she thinks that I am not judging her for having those beliefs, she begins to confide in me about her encounter with supernatural forces and fears, even mentioning some of the "evilous" people's names. She is very dramatic as she explains to me what these encounters are like. She opens her eyes wide, jumps out of her seat, points to her head, her stomach and her back, to show me the areas of her body that the spirits attack. Ariana finds it acceptable to state that she has had supernatural encounters, but that being a Christian woman, it isn't acceptable to state that she visits the healer whom she refers to as the *maddah woman* (mother woman) for help. She downplays her visits to the maddah woman by stating that at times she does not believe in those things, or that the maddah woman is her uncle's wife whom she often visits. Notwithstanding this, she constantly complains to me about the medical staff not allowing her to use her consecrated oil which she recounts is used by the maddah woman. Ariana also mentions that the oil that she is referring to is one that she got from one of the church sisters (James et al. 2013, 253). Oils (including olive oil) are typically used in Christian religious and traditional practices to anoint and heal the sick (Nji 2018).

Dre

Dre is a nineteen-year-old male from a lower-class socio-economic background and resides in an urban area. He is slim built, approximately 5 feet 2 inches in height and of dark complexion. He is dressed in a brown and blue plaid shirt and blue jeans and always wears his baseball cap which covers his eyes. He is diagnosed with schizophrenia and has been coming to the ward to receive treatment from the psychiatrist. However, Dre has a different explanation for his condition (James et al. 2013, 253) which does not entail chemical imbalance. He comes to my office and we both walk to the interview room. As we walk, he inquires how I am doing and what the agenda is for today. His voice is captivating and I can tell that he was schooled. He later informs me that he is a college dropout.

Dre sits in the chair next to the window. He slumps down in a comfortable position and looks up at me from beneath his baseball cap. As the interview begins to unfold, he changes his position, this time facing the window. I direct my attention to where he is looking, and I can see outside – the sky, the trees, and the mountains. I have not paid much attention to this throughout the time that I have been using this interview room. I decide not to interrupt as he stares outside at nature, telling his story. I join the process and we both venture on the journey of his past.

His voice is soft, calm and kind. He reminds me of an old wise storyteller. His narratives are so detailed that it is difficult for me not to visualize what he is describing. When I ask him the questions, he holds his head down, gazing on the floor and listens intently. After I am through with the question, he pauses. There is silence in the room. He strokes his small beard, his head moving as if he is nodding. He lifts his head up and looks through the window and, in a calm, but powerful voice, he captures my attention. My ears are alert. I feel like a young child in awe and filled with excitement waiting for the next series to unfold. There is an unspoken understanding that he can sense my excitement. He waits for me to compose myself, so as to allow me to be fully engaged with him on this journey. Although his descriptions of hell, fire and fear are vivid, and might appear to be a terrifying experience, Dre exudes confidence that he is spiritually equipped to handle the work of the devil. I am so engrossed with his story that I am only brought back to reality when he stops and asks me for water. I quickly give him the water which he sips, and continues, each time looking through the window, almost as if we are both seeing his lived experience.

Fiona

Fiona is a twenty-seven-year-old mother of two children, from a low socio-economic background and resides in a deep rural area. She is approximately 5 feet tall, medium built and of dark complexion. Her face is round and she has a nose that is slightly flat. She has a pleasant smile. Her eyes are small and dark brown and when she gets excited you can see the gleam in her eyes. Fiona is dressed in a brown skirt and matching blouse. After the birth of her last child, she was diagnosed with postpartum depression with psychotic features. She attends the clinic for her monthly appointments for what she considers to be a "nerves" condition. She is one of the first to arrive for her morning appointment and sits outside the outpatient facility on one of the benches. I look at her sitting with the other patients, her hands clasped and placed between her legs, and she has a look of contentment on her face. I later learn from Fiona in our interview that her "nerves" problem was related to stress and overwork and that she was not comparable to the patients she was sitting with as they were suffering from mental illness. I call her by her name; she answers and gets up proudly. She looks at the other patients, smiles and walks in my direction. She follows me into the interview room.

Fiona sits in her chair and leaning forward she begins unbraiding her hair. Fiona goes quickly and easily into her experiences with the spirits. I assume that given the way in which she relates to me, she feels that I understand the impact of the spiritual world. As this interview is taking place in rural Jamaica where the belief in spirits is widely accepted, it is not unusual for her to hold this perception. Fiona has recently lost her mother and stepfather and is haunted by their presence. She is a hard worker, a caring mother, who tries to give her eldest child guidance. She reports to me that she teaches him the principles of God and respect. However, she is concerned about him, as he lives with his father and father's girlfriend. She tells me that his step-mother isn't treating him well. Fiona is sad because she cannot provide for him. She also questions the fidelity of her current baby father. However, she tells me that he cares deeply for her and says that she must not listen to the rumours she is hearing. When she first started to feel the spirits, she went to a maddah woman who told her it was her baby father who has another baby mother and that this baby mother was setting spirits on her. She hisses her teeth and says, "Is a whole bag of foolishness she tell me" (She told me a lot of things that were not accurate). Fiona describes to me her different trips to various healers to get answers. She finally found one who was able to help her, which resolved the problems she has with the spirits.

She embraces her independence and becomes ashamed when she becomes sick with the nerves and others have to help her to do her chores. After learning how stress can "shatter her nerves", she currently tries to do less and takes a positive view of her situation. She relies on God for refuge despite her concerns that her baby father is cheating on her, financial difficulties and duppies (ghosts) trying to take her pretty baby.

Thomas

Thomas is a twenty-four-year-old male from a lower-class background and resides in a deep rural area. He is casually dressed in a t-shirt and dress pants. His complexion is dark, he is slim built and approximately 5 feet 10 inches in height. His eyes are bright, and he has a pleasant smile which remains constant throughout our interview. He is currently unemployed and lives with his mother and older brother. After he is finished with the nurse, he comes to my cubicle, smiles, and calls out to me. He is happy that I am back from "UC" (a common abbreviation for the University Hospital dating from when the university was a university college) because he enjoys our conversation.

I indicate that he should come in and he sits quickly on the chair. He comments on my beauty and tells me he is happy to be speaking with a beautiful girl. He tells me that girls won't take him seriously. He shares with me that the label of "mad man" follows him, because when he approaches girls, they soon discover his diagnosis and will not speak to him again. Although Thomas has the need for a relationship, he seems to have developed an aversion to women and finds evidence to support his theory. He tells me of his friend who turned mad because of a girl who looked just like me. According to Thomas, this girl broke his friend's heart by ending the relationship and migrating. After telling me about his friend's situation, he becomes serious and asks me to start the interview. He becomes more relaxed in the interview as I listen to his encounter with the different spirits. He tells me that when he tells people they don't believe him and they think that he is smoking weed (marijuana), especially when they see how red his eyes are. Thomas explains this redness to be as a result of the spirit possession. He tells me that when the spirits start acting up, he becomes very violent. No one can control him, and he becomes extremely strong.

Currently, Thomas has three spirits on him – one which he got from trying to find treasure. In his treasure hunt, he hit a pyramid which he should not have done, and the spirits came on him. The other spirit he got when he went outside of his home and a fallen angel came from the sky and hit him on his head. The third he got when he was fighting with a man over a piece of land and the man tried to keep him from this land by placing the spirit on him. Thomas has tried different healers and while some have worked temporarily, others have not. He believes that the most powerful healers are the ones from Antigua. He is currently waiting to get help from the spiritual people, but in the meantime, he is getting medication from the outpatient facility. He tries not to act like the other "mad people" as he stays "conscious" (on the right track) and drinks his natural herbal remedies to settle his nerves.

CHAPTER 4

"May I Speak to You?"

Openness and Understanding

WHEN I FIRST STARTED THIS JOURNEY, I STRONGLY believed that patients, in particular the ones who felt that their illness is caused by the supernatural, were advocating for the use of traditional medicine. Was I correct? And what did the Western practitioners think about these beliefs in the supernatural?

Early on in this book I had established that Western practitioners do not typically entertain discussions about Obeah and demon possession on the psychiatric ward. As Western practitioners, we seemed to have all adhered to these rules; science does not usually support such beliefs. My classmates, having realized that I was interested in studying Obeah informally told me of instances when they heard patients on the ward talking about Obeah being the main reason for their illness. Outside of them informing me of these events, my classmates and I have never really had a discussion about not engaging patients in talks about Obeah.

Having lived in Jamaica where conversations about Obeah and spirits are common (Beaubrun 1966; Weaver 2003; Hickling and James 2008), I often wondered what would be the case if Western practitioners were more sensitized and open to discussing traditional medicine with our patients. My thoughts were resolved after I conducted interviews with thirty Western practitioners, which included psychiatric nurses, psychiatrists and psychologists. These Western practitioners acknowledged that traditional medicine does play a major role in the lives of their patients and that often their patients wanted to have discussions with them about spirits and traditional medicine (James and Peltzer 2012).

The Western practitioners, however, admitted to not wanting to engage in these discussions with patients, as they had no confidence in the methods of traditional medicine and viewed it as a disservice to patients. According to the Western practitioners, when patients spoke to them about Obeah and spirits, they found that the patients became more distraught and anxious. They indicated, however, that they would become more open to the patients' desire to use traditional medicine if this approach met three criteria: (1) it is subjected to the rigours of the scientific method; (2) there is physiological proof of it being helpful to patients; and (3) they themselves have had personal experience (James and Peltzer 2012). This is understandable, considering that Western medical practitioners are trained based on the scientific method and will consequently have difficulty accepting a process that is not supported by empiricism and logic.

Irrespective of whether or not we engage patients in these discussions or find this approach to be useful, it is important to note that patients do seek help from traditional practitioners, and some do strongly believe that the supernatural is the cause and remedy of their illness. Therefore, Western practitioners' perceptions of traditional medicine and the role it plays in treating mental illness become vital if they are to have an impactful relationship with their patients. I wanted to have a better understanding of the Western practitioners' perceptions of the different types of traditional practitioners that were included in my study. Were their views the same irrespective of the type of practitioner, whether traditional healer, herbalist or alternative medicine practitioner? The findings from the interviews revealed that Western practitioners' views varied. While they had strong beliefs that traditional healing and herbs would have a negative impact on the patients, they were somewhat more open to alternative medicine. However, despite their comparative openness to alternative medicine, there was still hesitation (James and Peltzer 2012).

The practitioners indicated that they were not very knowledgeable about traditional medicine and the type of methods to which their patients may have been exposed. Interestingly, despite being underinformed and not convinced of the efficacy of traditional medicine, the Western practitioners were open to learning more about these methods (James and Peltzer 2012). Being open to learning, although an essential first step, does not equate to actively seeking out the information and none of the practitioners indicated that they took the initiative to acquire this information on their own.

For years psychiatric patients have attributed their illness to the supernatural. Despite this, very little work has been done on the effects of traditional medicine on patient care (Wedenoja 1983; Wittkower 1970; Weaver 2003). I was curious; what exactly are the methods that the traditional practitioners use? Why do the patients who seek help from them seem to have confidence in their approach? I wanted to learn more about the roles of spirits and how this impacts health.

To get this information, I visited both inpatient and outpatient psychiatric facilities. Like in any other waiting area at the hospital, patients sat quietly for their appointment. The patients generally seemed open to speaking with me. I was curious about this openness; I wondered how often researchers or other persons outside of their health-care team approached patients who have been diagnosed with a psychiatric illness. I also wondered if what I was seeing was evidence of the stigma of mental illness. Our patients would frequently communicate to us that when society learns that they have a psychiatric illness, they are often not taken seriously, and their voices are soon ignored. With these thoughts in mind, I wanted to ensure that I did not ignore the patients and their perspectives and focused my attention on capturing every detail each patient was willing to share with me. I introduced myself and told them about my study, I inquired if they would be willing to speak with me about their illness. The majority were welcoming and seemed curious about what I wanted to learn. I spoke to each patient in a private space and over the next few months I was able to record all sixty individual stories.

These stories contained patients' accounts of their illness, how it affected them, what they thought was the cause, what they did to help themselves as well as what they thought about the treatment they received. I must admit that from my perspective patients seemed to have had a positive experience from the interview. As the interviews unfolded, investment in the process seemed to grow. It was as if they were finally being able to share their story, they were finally being heard. This was more evident for patients who believed their illness to be caused by the supernatural. For me, this experience was also intriguing; my thirst to hear about the patients' views on the supernatural was finally being quenched.

When patients spoke about the supernatural, I noticed that their responses varied. Some seemed calm and in control while others were fearful and anxious. Based on their accounts, the ones that were calm had received confirmation that the illness was caused by supernatural forces and had gotten a resolution from the traditional practitioner on how to cope. Others who believed that their illness was caused by the supernatural but were fearful also felt that persons were actively using spirits to cause harm to them. These patients who expressed fear, did not want to delve into a lengthy discussion on the supernatural. They seemed to think that even making mention of spirits would summon them to action. Having seen their reaction, I understood that this might have been one of the reasons Western practitioners avoided speaking about the supernatural. This pointed to the fact that mention of supernatural forces might bring up disruptive feelings of fear in patients who were already struggling cognitively and emotionally. While this might have been a negative outcome of them sharing with me, I was grateful for their openness and courage to share their experiences. This openness and courage also convinced me that there was something about this interaction that helped the patients.

Inasmuch as I sensed the benefits, I questioned if I were correct: What exactly was beneficial for the patients? Was having a listening ear to talk about spirits in a Western setting beneficial to them? Or was it the fact that they were able to explain to me some of the methods used by the traditional practitioner and which was useful to them?

Listening is vital for a helpful relationship, especially when we are listening and acknowledging the sufferings of others. As practitioners, we understand the devastating effects of a mental illness and the ways it affects our patients' ability to function in all spheres of their lives. Although we work tirelessly to help our patients regain normality, we must realize that the patients are the ones that experience the illness and, therefore, are likely to be invested in their recovery. Whenever we as humans are faced with a challenge in life, we try to make sense of it by first labelling and then identifying its causes before eventually attempting to fix it. Naturally it is expected that in dealing with a mental illness, a similar approach will be taken to have it resolved. The conceptualization of the illness, whether it be biological or supernatural, will determine the type of help that patients seek.

There seem to be two main approaches taken by patients. There are those who seek help only from the Western practitioner and those who also seek help from the traditional practitioner. The patients who also seek help from the traditional practitioner are likely to be more inclined to believe that their illness is caused by spirits and therefore have a different worldview from their Western practitioner. If the worldviews are the same, then one would not anticipate any disharmony and the treatment agreed on will align for both the patient and the practitioner. If the worldviews oppose each other, then there will be discord and the likelihood of resistance to the treatment of the practitioner.

In order to understand the relationship between patients and practitioners, it makes sense to start at the beginning and get a sense of how the patients labelled their experience. All patients acknowledged having a problem or an illness; however, they typically avoided naming it as a psychiatric illness. In fact, they actively denied having a psychiatric illness. However, a small fraction admitted to their problem being psychiatric in nature (James and Peltzer 2012). For those who did not label the experience as psychiatric, there was a myriad of other explanations. Some referred to the problem as stress or just an illness, while other patients felt it was due to a demonic or super-natural attack. Regardless of their acceptance or rejection of a psychiatric diagnosis, the patients seemed to be in a state of desperation. They indicated that their major fear was to be in the state of the illness forever or of others harming them; a few admitted to being afraid of harming others. Considering the fears that were expressed, I was able to understand how vital the role of the practitioners is to the patients and why they expressed a need for the practitioners to help them to obtain relief and make the situation better.

Most of the patients who also included traditional medicine in their treatment indicated that they would like to talk to the Western practitioner about spirits and traditional medicine, but this was not entertained (James and Peltzer 2012). For these patients, this seemed to have caused some disharmony in the relationship between them and their Western practitioner. Their experience with the traditional practitioner, on the other hand, was different. Patients expressed that the traditional practitioner took the time out to truly listen and help them make meaning and connections with their experiences. The approach of the traditional practitioners was centred on the patients. The data from the sixty psychiatric patients seem to point further to the fact that we are perhaps disconnected from understanding this part of their lives and, consequently, their total experiences. If we do not take the time out to listen to their own interpretation and make space for talks about the supernatural, then can we say we are serving them?

As Western biomedical practitioners, we have undergone years of training to serve our patients and are equipped with scientifically sound skillsets. We administer medicine and/or psychotherapy and yes, thus far to some extent, these methods have proven to be successful. While this may be the case, there have been some grumblings from our psychiatric patients about the service we provide. These grumblings may be indicative of us missing a key component, one that seems to be vital to our patients. It seems that most of the patients who have also accessed traditional medicine are pleading with us to give them a response, to pay attention to their desire to speak about the supernatural and to take care to hear about their experiences with the traditional practitioner.

CHAPTER 5

Intersubjective Truths

REASONS FOR GOING TO THE PRACTITIONER

Noel has been diagnosed with paranoid schizophrenia by his attending psychiatrist. Noel's account of his experience of schizophrenia is as follows:

> The madness was still going on. I think for the whole day I just kept praying and that is what frightened my family . . . like they would see me being all frantic and praying and they would say, "What the hell is going on with this boy?" It was just pure madness basically. Madness on top of madness. And then I went to see [the doctor] and then he was just saying . . .

Noel's use of the term "madness" and the way in which he expresses it is important. Generally, we tend to think of madness as something that is "incomprehensible" (Van Dongen 2003, 207), an act which is outside the norm. Noel's descriptions are based on his own experiences. For him, madness is an intense ongoing process; one that is outside of his control. For the majority of us, for the most part we demonstrate a sense of control over our behaviours. In the brief moments when we act outside of how we know ourselves to be, we try to make sense of it, feel misaligned and if we are honest, we may admit to feeling embarrassed. We therefore may quickly get back to our typical behaviours. In the case of Noel, I empathize with what this must be like. Unlike the brief moments that most of us experience, for the person experiencing psychosis, the time frame is longer and the effort to regain normality seems relentless. It seems in Noel's case that he felt helpless to centre himself to normality and therefore had to cling to something more powerful such as his faith.

The individual who becomes ill is not the only one to be affected, but by extension, so too is his family. Witnessing a loved one losing control and trying to make sense of it also places the family in a helpless position. Unfortunately, and perhaps instinctively, this discomfort drives families to demand that their loved ones regain normality. In the case of Noel's family their response – "What the hell is wrong with this boy?" – gives the impression that his actions are within his control. Hidden within Noel's expression of "madness on top of madness" was his understanding that while he was experiencing his "madness", the family was mad to think that he had control over the situation. Noel, the one experiencing the psychotic episode, recognizes that it is out of his control, and while this is his own burden to bear, he suffers an even greater burden when his family articulates this unreasonable demand – that he should regain control.

I recognize through Noel's description the extent to which he found the experience frightening for him and also for his family members. One of the major flaws of the psychiatric diagnosis is that it does not give a detailed description of what the patient's experience is. Instead we are provided with a list of symptoms, as indicated by the *Diagnostic and Statistical Manual* (DSM-IV-TR) (American Psychiatric Association 2000).

For my own purposes, I need to understand Noel's experience in light of his emotional response to the events which he finds "frightening, frantic". He recognized that praying was not helping him to overcome his problem. It appears that although he was in the midst of this experience, he was try-ing to find the root of the problem and a solution for it. In recognizing that praying was not helping, he found another medium, such as the psychiatrist, to help him solve it. By going to the doctor Noel is already stating that he is not well. He is demonstrating his ability to recognize that his behaviour is outside of the norm and that it is causing distress to himself and others. It is this insight into his problem that led him to the doctor's office in the first instance.

Each individual is unique, and although Dre is also diagnosed as paranoid schizophrenic, he speaks about a different experience from Noel's.

> The devil is trying to destroy my life, not wanting me to succeed. With every episode I have it's a greater battle, a greater fight, it increases every time. It's like, for the first time you have a flu and you just get over it in a couple of days, but you know every time it happens the flu is transformed in asthma and bronchitis. I start out with tiredness, start out like nervousness, all of that. I am not usually a nervous person per se, and then after a while it get so intense so that it impairs your mental function and also your physical life. Mentally, there is like chaos in the mind, upheaval of some kind, like confusion; like you having hurricane, earthquake all sorts of things going on in your mind. It's just worse than a migraine. . . . I came to the ward and explain to them what was going on. From a medical perspective, they explained to me that was schizophrenia. (James et al. 2013, 254)

While Dre may have had a different experience, both he and Noel share similarities in their experience of a psychotic episode. Both Dre and Noel indicate that it took them by surprise. Dre equates it to a natural disaster, which indicates its unpredictability and its frightfulness. It is evident that in experiences such as these, individuals actively try to regain control of what is happening to them. The effort which each individual has to make to be able to regain control, seems incessantly exhausting – a "battle" or another "bigger hurdle" to overcome. Dre indicates that this force is an overwhelmingly negative force, which he believes has to be the devil's attempt to destroy his life. It seems that one way to regain control is to make sense of what is happening to you. Dre's attempt is shown here when he acknowledges the medical perspective. He, however, hints at his non-acceptance of the medical conclusion as he has a diagnosis of his own.

Control can take the form of an internal struggle, or it may be external, as is reflected in the case of Ariana where her struggle for control was between her and her doctor:

> Dr Maby admitted me and told me that I going to spend three days on the ward because my husband goes to work, the children goes [go] to school, so I honestly could not stay at home alone. And I know that I could stay there alone and I know I could stay, yu nuh [you know]. He seh that by Monday. By Monday he did not come and discharge me, so I tek up my bag and gone . . .

[He said that by Monday. By Monday he did not come to discharge me, so I took up my bag and left].

Lo and behold I see her coming into church [Actually, I see her coming into the church]. I seh "I worshipping [I said to her, "I am worshipping]. What is it?" If I can spare her one minute out of church? I seh no! [I said no!] She go to pastor's wife cause pastor's wife don't know that much about me, u nuh, cause is not that church I go to [She went to the pastor's wife, but the pastor's wife does not know that much about me, you know, because this is not the church I go to]. So they want to bond [bind] me to injection. Once a psychotic, always a psychotic. Although I told her the psychiatrist up by Cayman did a thyroid function test, and the thyroid function test seh [says] that I have hypothyroidism so is it triggering off the mental illness. I know I have to read that over cause I don't understand that much. (James et al. 2013, 256)

The case for mental illness is usually made by the patient's reports and the doctors' diagnosis. While mental illness can be debilitating and difficult for the patient, it does not always consume all of their faculties all the time, as we can see from Ariana's case.

Ariana shows me that while she may be in distress because of her anxiety, she is still able to have some insight into her condition. Despite her hesitation, she respected the doctor's decision for her to be hospitalized until she had support at home. This reasoning demonstrates the fact that while she has a mental illness, it does not cloud all of her ability to understand her situation. This kind of patient insight is very important to the practitioner, as it is this linkage that can be used in treatment to help the patent to regain her connection with the reality that we call normal living.

It is clear that in this case Ariana felt that the practitioner had not made the best use of her time as she "took up her bag and left". She was expecting that Dr Maby would have come back at the appointed time and at least let her know what was happening. This did not occur. She reports that she waited and "by Monday he did not come to discharge me".

This situation is reflective of the real life in the ward setting. Patients at times perceive that the psychiatric practitioners undervalue their personhood and show minimal regard for their comfort, lifeworld and commitments outside the ward. The result is that this patient demonstrated her own agency and left. It is possible that had she been visited on the Monday as agreed, perhaps she would have seen the reason for staying longer, and the problem of trying to retrieve her from church would not have occurred. What it seems Ariana is expressing is the need for others to be sensitive to her feelings during treatment.

This case also demonstrates the fact that being admitted to the ward removes all normal social protective mechanisms. This patient went into the church, a well-established place of refuge, but was offered no protection in her symbolic place of safety. Ariana laments her fate. She is unable to carry out what is considered a fundamental and harmless activity like worship. Even this is denied when she becomes labelled as a psychotic. She is diagnosed as mentally ill, but one of her struggles seems to be to get beyond this diagnosis to be seen as a person, not as a label. In the psychiatric setting, however, Ariana believes she may not have as much autonomy in reclaiming who she is as a person. Her description of this experience is "once a psychotic always a psychotic". She understands in a fundamental way how her role has changed in society and how the resulting relationships also change.

This theme is supported by Parson's functionalist perspective on illness (in Gallagher, 1976) which he describes as a type of deviance. The individual who is ill has deviated from the norm and no longer is able to carry out his functions. He suggests that the medical practitioners' role is to validate the illness and so allow the individual to adopt new roles. Since Ariana has been diagnosed and admitted to the psychiatric ward, she now has new roles in society. There are new relationships to be applied to her, as in this case where she was not allowed to worship in peace. This speaks to the powerlessness and lack of agency in her life.

Ariana does not realize that her role has been changed by her admission to the ward and the diagnosis she has been given, and so she is still expecting to be accorded the same privileges as a person who has not been diagnosed and placed in treatment. Taking Parson's theory further, it seems clear that she will only be accorded her normal privileges when she has been treated and given a clean bill of health by the medical practitioner. Her story reveals that practitioners have the ability to relocate a person within their social environment, with all the attendant difficulties that go with this relocation. The individual is powerless to resist and has to relearn new roles in order to function effectively in society.

There is evidence from Western biomedicine that a thyroid malfunction can affect one's mood, so as it is very likely that the practitioner would have made these checks, Ariana's comment about her thyroid problem is not farfetched. This reinforces the point that a person with a mental illness does not cease to be a thinking, feeling human being by any definition. They may have difficulties in some of their domains of functioning, but still retain the state of personhood. Ariana understands what the doctor is trying to say but she does not have enough information, and so she says that she needs to find out more. This demonstrates that she may be having problems in one dimension but still retains the basic human need to understand and to seek information as she constructs her own understanding of her illness.

SUMMARY AND CONCLUSION

As expressed in the quantitative findings, the majority (forty-two out of sixty) explained that their reason for going to the practitioner was largely because they were unable to function. We see where Noel, Dre and Ariana give a detailed account of what it is like to be unable to function as they normally would, and how this impacts on their relationships. Recognizing the inability to function is just the first stage of the process. There is then an effort to label the experience so as to know the extent to which the problem can be controlled. Both Dre and Noel have begun to label their illness as supernatural in origin, which coincides with the label of twenty-one of the sixty participants in the quantitative findings. There are other participants who have refused to label their experience as being psychiatric. Perhaps this is in an effort to prevent experiences similar to those that Ariana described.

THEMES OF OPPRESSION

There seems to be a consensus that regardless of geographic or temporal location, individuals are not immune to displaying behaviours that are deemed to be psychotic in nature (Teuton, Bentall and Dowrick 2007). The use of the term "psychosis" is a Western concept, one that patients have been fighting persistently to change. I examine the meanings that the patients make of their experiences by listening to the reactions that they have towards the psychiatric diagnosis they are given. In order for me to do so I have to take a more analytic perspective, trying to place myself both within the patient experience and at the same time applying my understanding of the psychiatric condition. According to Ogden (1994), placing myself in the analytic role helps me to give meaning and understanding to the feelings of the individual being analysed. In honouring the individual's voice, I have to take each one out of the category "patient", and simply acknowledge that each has a voice and wishes to be understood from their own perspective and experiences.

These are Ariana's words: "I only get upset if somebody keep telling me I am mentally ill and know I am not mentally ill! . . . so they want to bond [bind] me to injection. Once a psychotic, always a psychotic" (James et al. 2013, 255). Ariana, the nurse practitioner, is schooled in Western medicine and familiar with its practices. Despite her clear understanding of the symptoms that would lead to the diagnosis of mental illness, she does not agree that her experiences can be classified as such. In refuting her diagnosis, she emphasizes that this "somebody" who keeps insisting that she is mentally ill is adamant. Her fear of identifying this person is possibly attributed to her being in the psychiatric setting, and her concerns that the Western practitioners may overhear her. Regardless of the fact that she is herself a Western practitioner, her status does not make her immune to the Western system. Once she enters the Western system, she is stripped of her title, labelled "patient", and expected to play the role. She shows anger and frustration as her attempts to rid herself of the mentally ill label are not entertained. Ariana gives insight that "a psychotic" only receives injections, negating all other types of treatment. Her use of the term "bond me to injection" gives the impression that there is no escape, and speaks to the overwhelming prevalence of the use of this type of treatment. In addition, it also speaks to an invasion of her body, especially given that she thinks that she does not need it. The use of the term psychotic is also significant as the concept leaves her feeling misunderstood and powerless, overshadowing how she actually sees herself.

Charlotte shares a similar experience: "Just because I believe that God exist (pause), just because I believe in negative energy vs. positive energy (pause) doesn't make me schizophrenic. And I'm not paranoid about it either, so therefore I cannot be a paranoid schizophrenic. It doesn't make any sense!" (James et al. 2013, 255).

Charlotte first indicates her faith in God which seems to be very important when defining herself. Her other thoughts of negative and positive energy therefore become justified, if these are seen through the lens of someone who believes in God. Charlotte highlights the conflict between her belief system and Western medicine. The expression of her beliefs becomes seen as symptoms which Western medicine classifies as paranoid schizophrenia. She pulls the term apart in her attempt to prove that her belief system is neither "paranoid" nor "schizophrenic". She notes that her beliefs go unacknowledged, except when they are used in her diagnosis. It seems as though she believes she has been ridiculed, which is difficult for her to comprehend. It is as if her faith has been discounted as being outside of normal reasoning.

Dre acknowledges how Western medicine can disregard one's belief system. However, his reaction to this is different from Charlotte's:

> The doctors say it was hallucination, but I know I wasn't hallucinating. For me, that was an encounter with some supernatural stuff. . . . To tell you the honest truth, I really don't think I have an illness, because of how the spiritual aspect of life [connects to] the physical aspect of life. I understand that because of this spiritual experience it leaves physical marks. That's where the doctors come in. They treat whatever marks, whatever scars exist. (James et al. 2013, 258)

SUMMARY AND CONCLUSIONS

In the quantitative findings, patients visit practitioners with some amount of expectation. More than a half of the patients (thirty-four out of sixty) want the Western practitioner to make the situation better. Patients seem to be more specific in terms of what they are expecting from the traditional practitioner than from the Western practitioner, and the majority (twenty-two out of thirty) who also accessed traditional medicine, want to be freed from spiritual torment. It seems as though when patients view their illnesses differently from the practitioner, then there is a conflict with the patients' expectations and a conflict between both perspectives.

This conflict, as discussed by Charlotte and Ariana, results in some amount of distress, where they feel unheard and not able to give feedback to the treatment process. Unlike Ariana, Dre is not afraid to speak directly to the "doctors" when he discounts their diagnosis of his experiences as hallucination. His understanding of his experiences is based on the premise that the supernatural and the physical world are connected. Dre gives a description of his own worldview – of the connection between and consequences of these two merging worlds. He highlights his battle with the supernatural forces and its traces in the physical world as evidenced by the scars he has. Dre displays a gentle and confident persona and is quite convincing with his arguments. His belief resonates strongly in him. It seems as if he refuses to engage in another "battle" with Western practitioners to prove that his beliefs are genuine. It appears that he gets what he sees as naïve doctors, to be engaged in and indirectly reiterate his spiritual experience when they treat his physical scars.

Causes and Cures

The participants' accounts of their diagnostic labels indicate that each has been placed in a category that results in their identities being lost. It is therefore crucial for me to highlight what each individual is fighting against. There is Ariana, the psychotic; Dre, hallucinating; and Charlotte, the paranoid schizophrenic. In my interviews, they strongly refused to be labelled with a diagnosis. Rather, each highlighted different causal pathways to their experiences which did not involve being mentally ill.

There is much to be learned from these responses. First, these informants refused to play the role of the psychiatric patient. Their resistance to these labels indicates that they are not passive when it comes to their treatment, and each rejects the practitioners' interpretation of their experience. In resisting the role of the practitioner, Ariana, Charlotte and Dre exert their sense of self. Despite their efforts, they are neither heard nor understood, which results in anger, frustration, a sense of helplessness and defeat. I am able to use their narratives, their emotional reactions, and put myself in each individual's position to experience (*verstehen*) what it must be like for the patient. This results in me finding the *essence* of what a psychiatric diagnosis means for each participant. In this instance, that essence speaks to a feeling of being oppressed.

Mishler (2005, 433) highlights the belief that the patient-physician relationship can be one that is oppressive. He implies that medicine might be viewed as an "oppressive social institution". It therefore stands to reason that these individuals first have to cope with the disruption in their lives caused by the particular phenomenon that is "spirits", or however they may conceptualize it. Second, in an environment that should be a part of the resolution, individuals have to battle the oppressor in claiming their right to express their understanding of their own experiences. To further reiterate this point, Mishler (2005) also expresses ethical concerns about the exclusion of informants' personal accounts of illness experiences in understanding and managing their symptoms, complaints and illnesses in the places where they go for help (hospitals, clinics, physician offices). It is not surprising, therefore, that the patients would express dissatisfaction with the care they receive from doctors and other health-care providers. Patients' major complaints are that physicians do not value their own reasons for being ill, nor do they take time to listen.

THE CLASH BETWEEN RELIGION AND WESTERN BIOMEDICINE

Throughout the interviews with the participants, the first refuge that they seek in dealing with the mental illness is usually to cling tightly to their religious beliefs. It seems that from a religious standpoint, in making sense of their situation, participants conceptualize their illness as being from an outside source, not coming from within. The healing or remedy for the illness, however, comes from God, which patients seem to believe comes from within themselves. In my interview with Noel, he gives a brief synopsis of his religion: "Well, personally, I've always been taught that there is God. He has his angels. Some angels rebel against him. There is a ring-leader called Satan, you know, and then these are evil forces that torment people. Basically, they do the opposite of what's right and they sometimes torment people."

Noel highlights his religious background. This makes me reflect on his upbringing of having been exposed to two distinct religious denominations in his family. He presents this as conflict within his family, with one religious denomination being right and the other being wrong. This shows his alliance with one side of the family, which becomes a part of his identity. He takes ownership of the knowledge he obtained about God and Satan, which appears to be important in defining himself. In his hierarchy, he identifies God as the head, the person who does right. Noel equates his normal functioning to being good, which therefore must be the work of God through him. On the other hand, he sees his illness as an outside force, the devil, and not something that is a part of him. Despite having God within him, he expresses fears and helplessness when the demon enters and possesses him.

Ariana expresses the same sentiments as Noel and describes her experiences with evil as follows:

> Mi nuh like talk bout De Laurence [American publisher and author known for occult theories and novelties popular in Jamaica and the Caribbean (Cassidy and Le Page 2002)] you know, cause is someting dreadful [I don't like to talk about De Laurence, you understand, because it is something that is dreadful]. . . . De Laurence is dangerous people. Dem dangerous . . . evil powas [They are dangerous . . . evil powers]. Dem av high powers [They have high powers]. . . . If you working with them, then them don't trouble you; but dem [they] have high powers . . . you have De Laurence, you have Negromancy [black magic, possibly corruption of necromancy], you have Obeah [use of spells witchcraft/ sorcery to harm others], you have witchcraft; four of them you know, but four different sinting [things].

According to Ariana, evil forces are extremely powerful. In discussing this she becomes aware of her present situation and the negative impact that De Laurence has on her life. Ariana is protective of her internal world. Her fear of mentioning the name of this famous and powerful occult practitioner indicates that by virtue of even mentioning the name, the internal world therefore becomes vulnerable to the influence of what is believed to be the strongest of all evil spirits. Calling the name can place her in tremendous danger. In addition, she is also battling with her concern for herself as she was told by the healer that this was the spirit that was affecting her. There are the social implications, as, by putting the evil of De Laurence on her, the tenacity of the malicious intent of those who wish to harm her is evident.

Ariana shows throughout the interview that she identifies with the Christian faith which goes against the work of De Laurence. This is an important piece of information as she mentions that a person would only be in danger if they opposed the evil forces. This puts her at even more risk. She also points out that if you work with evil, evil will not harm you. It is clear that she is working against evil forces, which makes her more vulnerable to attack by evil spirits which could possibly be the four different types she mentioned.

Whereas Ariana feels that she could go no further in her explanation of the evil spirits because she had mentioned their names, Dre was able to give me more insight into the difference between good and bad spirits:

> If you understand how God operates, God is not going to give you sickness. God don't operate like that. Sickness is not from God because the Bible says that he wishes you to prosper and . . . be in good health. So if he desires that, why would he want to bring sickness on you? So the devil realizes this, and he is going to do a lot of things in his power, a lot of sickness, whatever he wants to do he is going to do it. His purpose is to steal, kill and destroy, whatever he has to do. If it is mental illness, AIDS, if it is cancer, whatever he wants to do. But if you are firmly rooted in God or in Christ then the devil cannot touch you, you know. The devil can't touch you unless God wants it to happen.

Dre believes that it is important to appreciate the teachings of God as it relates to sickness and health. In taking on the role of a teacher in our discussion, he shows that he has deep understanding of these principles. His introduction of the Bible – "the Bible says" – speaks to not only his relationship with this book but also the life that he gives this book – almost as if it were a person who speaks. He separates God from the devil and teaches me about each. Dre indicates that naturally God wants us to prosper and have good health. The devil, however, in knowing that we have the desire to prosper, tries to take away from us what God has in store, by bringing sickness; and this could come in any form, sickness of the mind, such as mental illness, or sickness of the body, such as cancer. After giving me this lesson, Dre informs me that if I want to be free from illness then it is important for me to hold on to these words. It is this faith that will prevent the devil from harming me. In essence, this understanding and acceptance would not result in me questioning myself when I see the work of evil. He insists that it is all about my mindset. If I focus on the sickness, then I am questioning what God has in store for me. If I hold on to the thoughts that God only wants me to be healthy, then I will be healthy, and the work of the devil will not take effect.

At this point, the general consensus among the patients I interview is that sickness is caused by the devil and the way to get rid of this is to both align with God and believe in God. It seems as though if one should mention or think about the works of evil, then evil will manifest itself. It is therefore important not to give any attention to evil, but to focus on good. The literature, though limited, has also shown instances where the mental health problem is believed to be understood as being caused by Satan and the devil, and alleviated by the divine power of the Holy Ghost, through prayer, singing, receiving holy water and laying on of hands (Teuton, Bentall and Dowrick 2007; Griffith 1983).

I am pleased that the participants are able to share their understanding of the spiritual world with me. There are varying degrees of comfort when they speak about good and evil. When discussing good, they are able to speak more comfortably, while evil seems to bring more discomfort. I note this more in Ariana and to a lesser extent in Noel. Dre seems to have more control over the situation, and it seems as if this is based on his understanding of the Christian principles and on the faith to which he holds. He did not display this fear because of his belief that in identifying with God and holding true to this belief, evil spirits could not bring any harm. Ariana's anxiety, on the other hand, had much to do with her concentration about not being on the side of the evil spirits and the implications that this would have for her. From this information I could get a sense of the strength of each individual when faced with evil forces.

BAD MIND, OBEAH, RED EYE: DISHARMONY IN RELATIONSHIPS

The first encounter with the spiritual as being the cause of mental illnesses was found in the quantitative findings. The overall findings indicate that a total of 27 out of 60 believed that their illness was caused by the supernatural and 44 out of 60 believed that someone or something could perform Obeah. Fiona, Ariana, Thomas and Dre give detailed descriptions of the impact of the spiritual world and its impact on sickness which was mentioned briefly in the explanation of good and evil. Their narratives illustrate the role of culture in their worldviews. Understanding the role of culture here is critical because only then will we understand how patients conceptualize their illness and treatment. The literature gives more depth and clarity to this issue by highlighting that individuals, in understanding their illness, will place it in the category of either the natural or supernatural. The natural causes are recognized by Western biomedical sciences – such as infection, stress, or organic deterioration. The supernatural is bound up in the African people's interpretation of health and disease (Edwards et al. 1983). The supernatural is usually more reflective of the layperson's experience of health and illness, and their ideology is usually congruent with their values (McClean 2003).

Africans tend to display the belief that it is not uncommon for individuals to become ill due to the malicious intent of others who use magic to harm or injure their victims (Edwards et al. 1983). The belief in witchcraft and sorcery as the cause of illness has captured the attention of many researchers. Most social anthropologists suggest that this is key in understanding African social life. Some have taken the functionalist approach by explaining this as a means of individuals trying to maintain equilibrium by emphasizing the morale-sustaining and normative functions of life. Douglas (1970, cited in Corin and Bibeau 1980) indicates that the explanation of witchcraft occurs when social interactions are intense, and roles are ill-defined. Both Thomas and Fiona are able to shed light on conflicts in their social relationships and the role of the spirits in these conflicts. Thomas explains:

> Because as mi see di man weh ded im help trick mi tu [Because as I have seen the man who died, he was the one who helped to put trick on me too]. Because yu can use someting like bullfrogs – all dem stuff very evil – and dem ting yu know; and you can go to the graveside with your black book and raise up spirit [Because you can use something like bullfrogs-all these things are very evil-and these things you know; and you can go to the graveside with your black book and raise up spirits]. Him ded now still [He is now dead]. Trick is like you put on demons on yu, on people, understand? [Trick is when you put demons on people, understand?] . . . Me and the man was fighting over piece of land, see? After that, after him work him tricks and thing and me enter the land mi get sick [After that, after him work him tricks and thing and when I entered the land, I got sick]. Him say him ah go kill me; him must kill me [He said he was going to kill me; he must kill me]. And me and him nuh fight physically [He and I did not fight physically]. Is a spiritual thing him a try fi use pon mi cause mi say you have evil spirit [It is a spiritual thing that he tried to use on me, because I said you have evil spirit].

We see where Thomas's belief of the role of the supernatural in conflicts can have a powerful and lasting effect; even when his rival has died, the spirits cast what he refers to as "tricks", which still seem to be affecting his health. While Thomas may have had more control were this conflict a physical or verbal one, he demonstrates that when evil spirits are involved, one does not stand a chance. It seems Thomas, with this belief, has accepted his fate as one that is eternal.

Like Thomas, Fiona also makes reference to how the spiritual can affect one's health. She is of the opinion that the dead can cause harm:

> As mi go so di man tell mi seh is spirit [immediately when I went to the man, he told me that it was spirit]. "She don't want anything happen to yu; is yu madddda and yu stepfather. You madda don't want to do yu anyting. Di madda love unnu" ["She does not want anything to happen to you, it is your mother and stepmother"]. . . . Mi an wan a mi breddah couldn't [a]gree. Dat was the laas bredda; one son fi mi madda [My brother and I could not agree. That was the last brother]. Me an him hav a lot of quarrel and mi madda did love dat wan [He and I quarreled a lot and my mother loved him especially]. So mi wonder if is it cause di problem or wat [So, I wondered if that was what caused problem or what?]. . . . Di man nevah like mi wen him was alive. Him dead; him spirit don't like mi [The man never liked me when he was alive. He is now dead; his spirit does not like me]. Yes is spirits! Di first night dem went in di yaad and I know dem was dere. I feel dem [Yes, it is the spirits! The first night they went into the yard and I knew they were there. I could feel them].

Fiona shows faith in the healer. This is mainly because he immediately confirms her beliefs that the problem was spiritual in nature without her discussing it with him. This makes him seem even more knowledgeable and powerful. More so, he could accurately discuss the type of relationship Fiona had with her mother and stepfather. The healer highlights the importance of having good relationships with others as this has implications for how these individuals, when dead, would relate to one. Further, maintaining good balanced social relations is in keeping with the African belief to good health, the opposite of which can cause ill-health (Cocks and Møller 2002). Although Fiona knows that her mother loves her, her mother's spiritual appearance makes her question if she is upset with her because of the conflict she has had with her brother. Regarding the stepfather, it makes perfect sense that he would harm her, as he did not display any love for her when he was alive. If the relationship had unresolved conflict, when the person dies the spirit could return which could cause illness in the living – "him dead him spirit don't like me" (he is dead, his spirit does not like me). Fiona also speaks about the physical reaction that the spirits can evoke in the living – she can "feel" their presence.

The nature of social relationships seems to be a dominant theme when establishing the causes of illnesses. This is a reflection of an African retention; similar to how it is viewed in some places in Africa, one of the explanations provided for ill-fortune is the disruption in social relationships. When there is a disruption or conflict in a relationship, such as a grudge that someone may have, this can cause the person bearing the grudge to harm the other individual by using spirits. This is illustrated by Fiona and Ariana. First, Fiona says:

> Di same year wen mi pregnant, yu realize seh someting wrong [The same year when I got pregnant, I realized that something was wrong]. When mi pregnant, *wen I was lying in di bed* – di first time [When I was pregnant, when I was laying in the bed – the first time]. It was di very first time [It was the very first time]. After dat, a have di baby, two time; two time dem attack [After that, I had the baby, two times; two times they attacked]. Honesly, mi have on a guard ring, wen me carry back di baby to di same man [Honestly, I had on my guard ring, when I carried back the baby to the same man]. Im seh is di baby dem want [He said it they wanted the baby]. Seh di baby is veri pretty so dem want di baby [He said the baby is very pretty, so they would like to have the baby]. Im bathe down di baby [He gave the baby a special bath]. A don't know wat im use to do it [I don't know what he used to do it]. I see him mix up three tings an bathe down di baby an from dat until now mi alright [I saw him mix three things together and gave the baby a bath and from that time until now, I have been alright].

Fiona is aware of the changes that have taken place in her life, and these have aided her in her diagnosis of the problem. She indicates that the first time the spirits came was when she was in resting position. She indicates that their activities became more intense after the birth of her child, which is when they actually attacked, not once, but twice. She tried to assess the situation which did not make sense to her as she wore her guard ring (a ring used to ward off evil spirits) which was supposed to protect her. As is customary in African retention, the use of ornaments to protect self and family seems to play an important role. Additionally, the research also shows that infants are particularly vulnerable to harm from spirits. Fiona shows her faith in the healer who gave her this guard ring by returning to him to assess the situation, as it seemed to her that the spirits were after the baby, and she was formulating a diagnosis of her own. This self-diagnosis also confirms the approach taken in African culture; Fiona has already made her own assessment and seeks confirmation. Her faith in the healer is confirmed, as he was able to indicate that the spirits were indeed targeting the baby. Fiona is proud to inform me that the reason they wanted to take her baby was because of the baby's beauty, giving the impression that spirits liked to take pretty babies. Her not knowing what the healer placed in the bathwater speaks to the mystery of his practice. The literature shows that the efficacy of the traditional healer can be seen in the secrecy of his methods. This helps us to explain why she has even more confidence in the traditional practitioner's methods. She explains how everything has been alright since then, confirming that both she and the healer were right in their analysis of the situation. We see clearly in this situation that the healer is able to relieve her tension, which seems to have led to her gaining even more trust in his methods. She offers:

> Im read mi up and tell mi everyting [He gave me a reading and told me everything]. Im sit down and im light im candle an im say a psalm [He sat down and he lit his candle and recited a psalm]. . . . Im say di people in di district don't like mi [He said the people in the district do not like me]. Yes. Because honestly, from mi a grow up dem definitely don't like di family [Yes. Because honestly, from the time I was growing up, they definitely did not like the family]. Dem don't like di family [They don't like the family].

Fiona gives another explanation as to ways in which spirits can attack. Once again, she goes back to the explanation given to her by the healer. She is even more impressed with him because of his use of the Bible, confirming that what he is doing is good. It is not unusual for African traditional religious beliefs to also incorporate other religious elements as is seen here with the practitioner's use of Christian rituals (Pyne-Timothy 2002). It seems as though the healers sought by Fiona have all incorporated some religious element in the diagnosis of her problem. Fiona's last visit to the healer not only confirmed her belief that her problem was caused by spirits but also that she had problems in her social environment. "Bad mind" and "red eye" are terms commonly used to express conflict in social relations in the Jamaican setting (Hickling and James 2012). "Red eye" refers to an individual who is jealous, angry and envious towards another person's achievements, while "bad mind" shows an evil intent. Having "red eye" means that jealousy is activated in the individual which may propel this individual to seek the help of the Obeah man to activate spirits to cause harm to the individual to which their jealousy is directed (Hickling and James 2012). Even though the terms "red eye" and "bad mad" were not directly used by Fiona's healer, he suggested this by highlighting that the underlying root of her problem is that the members in her community do not like her and they used spirits to express their dislike to Fiona.

Ariana's situation seems similar to Fiona's:

> They say Ariana, everybody wake you up. Why you don't wake up? Can't wake up; couldn't wake. So the invigilator say she try to wake me up too, but I couldn't wake [So the invigilator said she also tried to wake me up, but I could not be awakened]. To be honest, I was tinking bout wichcraft; the honest truth [To be honest, I was thinking about witchcraft; the honest truth] . . . yes, all my tutors wonder what it was because it is not like I know everyting [yes, all my tutors wondered what it was because it is not like I knew everything]; but I am brilliant. They wonder why I couldn't do my exam; um, dem used to call it someting like supastition [They wondered why I could not do my exam; um, they used to call it something like superstition].

Ariana shows how deeply she was sleeping – the sleep she believes was not a normal type of sleep as, despite the countless efforts of others to awaken her, she still remained asleep. In assessing the situation, she highlights her capabilities. She is brilliant; therefore, it could not be that she was unable to do her exam. She highlights how others could be envious of this brilliance and would try to put things in place so as not to make her succeed (this is another example of persons having "red eye" or "bad mind"). Ariana's assumption of her being brilliant and therefore the target of envy for harmful spells, is a commonly held belief in African retention as one of the main reasons behind harm being inflicted on others through the use of the supernatural (Cocks and Møller 2002). The fact that others agree with her analysis, makes her feel justified in thinking that someone was using witchcraft against her, which prevented her from doing her exam. For Ariana and others, it must have been the work of witchcraft, especially given that it was known that she was an intelligent person. This way of thinking highlights the deeply embedded African culture and its influence on health and wellbeing. Ariana further says:

> Somebody, lady who work at the hospital who is Christian, tell mi dat me madda gave me up as sacrifice [Someone, a lady who works at the hospital, who is a Christian, told me that my mother gave me up as a sacrifice] . . . sacrifice is someting like yu owe De Laurence an you hav to go [a sacrifice is something that is similar to you owing De Laurence and you have to go]; you hav to die [you have to die]. *But I shall not die! Live on the cradle peace of the Lord, amen!* I am not gonna let them kill me [I am not going to let them kill me]. If she put mi up for sacrifice that is fi her business. Is she ah go dead cause me nah go dead [If she puts me up for sacrifice that is her business]. I shall not die.

The theme of others using spirits to harm the participants in this study continues to be pervasive throughout the narratives. The messenger for Ariana is mysterious. Ariana does not find it necessary to give the person's name; however, she discloses an important piece of information – this person is employed at the hospital and is a Christian. This reiterates the point that individuals from a Christian background tend to be more credible. Ariana mentioned in our interview the difficulty she had in her relationship with her mother. She proudly spoke of her Christian faith and of other members in the family who were Christians; but she wasn't convinced that her mother was Christian because of her behaviour. The tension in their relationship, coupled with the unchristian-like behaviour, made it likely that her mother would give her up as a sacrifice to the devil. She, however, felt empowered with the support of other Christians, and fuelled with her anger towards her mother, she chose to fight her. In comparison to other times when she spoke about De Laurence, it seems as though she feels stronger mentioning his name at this point in the interview. In fighting her mother, it seems as though winning this battle would cause the spirits to go back to the mother who would succumb to the faith that she had placed on Ariana in the first place. Perhaps the strength that Ariana is feeling may also have to do with the fact that she believes she has identified the person who has caused her harm and in situations like these when the perpetrator has been identified (as is explained by Crawford and Lipsedge 2004), the victim now has the autonomy to reverse the perpetrator's spell. This, coupled with her religious faith, seemed to have given Ariana even more determination to fight through her challenges.

Despite hearing stories that the spirits can be sent by others, Dre sheds light on another perspective and informs me that evil spirits can act on their own accord, and are more likely to target individuals whom they believe are more spiritual. According to Dre, spiritual individuals are more susceptible to the works of the devil, as the devil places obstacles in their way to make it become even more difficult to grow spiritually. He elaborates: "The gift that I have spiritually, if used will have a great impact on a lot of lives and because you know, the devil knows that if I matured as a child of God and basically all these progresses. . . . I believe that I am being thwarted or perturbed from being able to accomplish what I am supposed to accomplish."

Dre believes that he has been blessed spiritually. He indicates that he has not grown fully in the spiritual dimension because of the constant targets set by the devil. He recognizes, however, that if he consistently fights this battle, he will eventually accomplish his ordained task.

Thomas adds to Dre's account:

> Those people see you have spiritual gifts; just like you go into church and you have the Holy Spirit, you get spiritual gifts – you get gifts from the spirit to heal people – see you go to church, and some people change and gone get wickedness [they go to get wickedness] – get spiritual gifts and them use it a different way by hurting people [get spiritual gifts and they use them it in a different way by hurting people] . . . because you can go to people and them mek you car tun over and crash if you nuh strong in yourself [because you can go to people and they can make your car overturn and crash if you are not strong within yourself]. If your spirit nuh strong enough, dem will kill you [If your spirit is not strong enough, they will kill you], cause it happen plenty up my way, all up in Somerset them mek the girl ah run up and down naked [because it happens a lot around my area of residence]. So you haffi fight and pray hard enough to fight the evil people. It happen to me [so you have to fight and pray hard enough to fight people who are evil].

Thomas educates me that the individuals who receive the spiritual gifts are the ones who go to church and have within them the Holy Spirit. The spirit itself gives the gift to heal. However, some tend to take the spiritual gifts to do harm and as such they stop going to church. They can destroy your life or property and make you lose your sense of self. One can overcome this by holding strong to one's faith and praying hard. Thomas shows me that this is not an easy battle, requiring a lot of work to overcome these forces. If one is not strong enough the result could be death.

INDIVIDUALS ARE SPIRITUAL BEINGS

In other instances, there is the belief that individuals are spiritual beings and can possess within themselves either negative or positive energy. A person brings along with them their particular energy which can contaminate anyone or anything around them. Charlotte gives an example of how this works:

> My sister came with her things. . . . I started, automatically I stopped working. . . . I stopped doing what. . . . I was in the process of writing a book . . . um, I had to stop writing the book. . . . She left a lot of the things there and it invaded everything; everything . . . the energy that was in my house that I needed to use to write my book . . . to . . . paint . . . to . . . write my songs, my music . . . um . . . all of those things, even dancing. A lot of times I dance in my house like for like exercise and therapy. I couldn't dance anymore and it's like my entire life . . . gone.

Charlotte describes the spiritual world and how in tune with it she is. It should be noted that here she refers to the spiritual world as energy. She can "automatically" detect any changes in the energy flowing through her home. A person can carry with them a particular type of energy which can be transmitted to their personal belongings. When energy from one person who is negative clashes with another person whose energy is positive, it impacts on the positive person's functioning. In illustrating positive and negative energy Charlotte points to the type of relationship she has with her sister and the need for her to separate herself from her. Given the sister's impact on her, this relationship seems to be intense. Charlotte speaks of her artistic abilities – writing, painting, music and dance – as though these are things that define her. If these were taken away, she could not be alive anymore. She speaks about the spiritual encounter which disrupted her usual daily activities.

Dre, on the other hand, gives detailed information about his spiritual encounter and how it impacted on him physically:

> I remember I was in this place and it was a hot dark place. I was tormented. I could feel fire. I could see images. . . . They were really dark, cold; something like what, almost like you see in the movies. But it is worse than what you see in the movies... for me that was an encounter with some supernatural stuff. . . . It was like the devil himself trying to kill me, trying to destroy me. I was sort of in a war, like warring for my soul. . . . This spiritual experience, it leaves physical marks. . . . The devil trying to destroy my life, not wanting me to succeed. . . . I wanted to be delivered. I wanted to get rid of what was plaguing me and as I got to the altar it happened. I went there, they were praying and going around and I got very upset for no apparent reason and I just started to back away; didn't want anyone to touch me. It was a rage inside . . . I like to think of it as being demonized.

The place that Dre speaks about does not have a name, which gives some mystery to it. He describes heat, darkness, fire, coldness and images. He tries to make me understand the terror that he felt, which he associates with scary movies. I can imagine being in a scary movie and this being my reality. My imagination of this makes me connect with the fear that Dre spoke about. His analysis of the situation is that it was spiritual in nature. Dre speaks about his battle with the devil and alludes to being demon possessed. He associates the devil with darkness, fire, and coldness, and confirms his belief when he went to the altar and the evil spirits started to rage within him. His use of strong words such as kill, war, plague, physical marks, depicts how intense this conflict is. Again, the issue of the battle of good versus bad resurfaces. Prayer itself counteracts the devil, even if it did not surface initially. Dre's narrative is in keeping with the findings of Rowe and Allen (2004), in that when there is ill health, individuals often rely on their faith to help them through these challenges.

Noel expounds on his reliance of prayer through his difficult moments:

> I guess I was having delusions, you know what I mean. Like I thought I was demon-possessed, basically. Like I would feel a certain – I would not say personality – but I would feel a certain feeling. Like I would hear myself cursing at God, but it would not really be me; and then it would worry me and then I would say to myself, "Wow; was that really me?" And now I would be in trouble

with God for doing that. And then I would get frighten and then I would have all the delusions about going to hell. And after that I heard my brain saying things that I was not in control of, you know what I mean; like really scary stuff. When I would hear these things I would get so frighten because I thought that I would be written off by God, and I would start tensing up and sweating and start getting frightened. I can't describe it better than me just going mad really. So I just started, started praying out loud, because in some way I believed I was demon-possessed, you know; so I believe I had to call on God, you know. . . . I kept on thinking that God is going to hold me responsible for something . . . cause the whole time my mind was saying, give in to these demons. I just kept thinking, shoot – what if I give in to them? God will never forgive me again, no matter what I do, you know what I mean? And I just kept thinking about burning in hell forever and just some really scary thoughts.

Noel utilizes the word delusion, a Western concept, to explain what he was experiencing. He, however, resorts to explaining this phenomenon through the use of terms that he understood at the time and was more familiar with. For Noel, demon-possession meant that there was another part of himself over which he had no control. Although the voice that he heard cursing at God was his own voice, he was careful to say that it wasn't a part of his personality, choosing to disassociate himself. His Christian background and principles made him become concerned, as this voice of his was going against everything that he had learned, and this was a terrifying experience for him. Noel expresses the view that if a person goes against God, this can result in God writing him off and sending him to hell. Noel has a difficult struggle. On one hand, there is the spiritual part of him, trying to gain control. On the other, there is another side of him convincing him that he should lose control. The thought of giving up and losing control brought about thoughts of condemnation.

The encounter with the spiritual world does not necessarily have to be confined to one's thoughts; but as Dre demonstrates, it can be through an actual physical experience.

Fiona is also of this belief as she relates to me how the spirits of her mother and stepfather affected her:

Mi mother and mi stepfather died [My mother and my stepfather died]. Then them come around, them come around and them give a lot of problems [Then they came around, they came around and they gave a lot of trouble]. Them [They] never used to give a lot of problem, the two of them up on the road [both of them were on the road]. . . . About 2001, mi feel them [I could feel them]. When them come around mi feel the heat [When they come around, I can feel the heat], and mi head raise, yea swell [and my head raises, yes it swells]. . . . Like on the whole a di inside, in ah mi stomach [Like the entire inside, in my stomach], turn out; and that time the man tell mi them fooling around with mi food [turns out; and that time the man told me they were fooling around with my food], mi dinner, like them a eat out mi inside; fire inside [my dinner, like they ate out my inside, fire inside].

The death of these people raises questions as to their impact on the living. It appears that they became more of a problem dead than when they were alive – speaking to the power of the spirits. It seems as though there was some anticipation of their arrival, and Fiona's belief can be supported when others see these spirits on the road. There are physical reactions to spirits coming around, which include heat, fire and the head being "raised" (that is, the spirits having a physiological impact). According to Fiona, spirits can be attracted to people if they have food in their stomachs. It is not just the food that they are interested in, but spirits can reach to the point where they can eat the entire inside, leaving a burning sensation.

FEAR

Right through the narratives the participants have indicated that their experiences, whether they be referred to as psychoses, delusions, evil spirits or by other terms, have resulted in a loss of control, where the sense of self has been taken over by another force that is unrecognizable. In trying to make sense of the loss of control, the participants' first line of reasoning is that this is due to spiritual or supernatural causes. This further intensifies the loss of control in the face of which they feel powerless. The emotion that best captures their experience is fear.

USE OF RITUALS TO COMBAT SPIRITS

Throughout the narratives the participants spoke about healers, their use of prayers, rituals and calling on God to help them to address the spiritual dilemma. In fact, twenty of the thirty participants who had visited the traditional practitioner agreed that the practitioner gave them clarity on their situation, and twenty-two of the thirty wanted him to use his rituals to get rid of the spirits that were harming them. Hamilton (1998) is of the belief that patients already have an unconscious archetype of who a healer is. Patients, he believes, attribute to the healer a more powerful and positive image than that of the modern physician. He cites and further elaborates on the work of Herbert Benson (1996), who made reference to the "remembered wellness" (20) which equates to the powerful expectations that patients have of healers. Remembered wellness therefore has a placebo effect, which stimulates the unconscious psycho/physical phenomenon, resulting in improved physical and emotional health. As an example, Arianna describes her experience:

> She anoint you with the olive oil and she will take something out of your head, out of your arm, and, you know... like some glass or something... glass bottle. And she use lime and she squeeze it and take out some glass. One of the time, she take out something from, I think it was here [Ariana points to her back] and she seh it look like some De Laurence work [and she said it looked like some De Laurence work]. Mi nuh like talk bout De Laurence you know [I don't like to talk about De Laurence, you know], cause is something dreadful that [because this is something dreadful]. De Laurence is dangerous people dem [De Laurence are dangerous people]; dangerous evil powers. Them have high powers so she say not to worry myself [They have high powers so she says not to worry myself]. Me must just pray; and she give me the bottle of oil [I should just pray; and she gave me the bottle of oil].

Ariana gives insight into the practices of the healer and her procedure in diagnosing the problem. The use of olive oil and lime and touching of the different body parts can be used to remove evil spirits. This practice seems common to nineteen of the thirty participants who also mentioned that their practitioner had utilized olive oil in treating their problems. It seems as though the olive oil gives the healer information as to where the spirits are, and the lime is used for the more rigorous work of removing objects from the body. Although my impression of the spirits is intangible, the De Laurence spirits, when removed from Ariana's body, manifest themselves in the tangible form of glass. For Ariana, evidence of the De Laurence spirits is proof that someone has placed witchcraft on her. Both the healer and Ariana seem to have the same view, in that Ariana mentions that she was afraid of De Laurence, and expresses her fear of just mentioning him in our interview. The healer, having found his work, knows its implications for Ariana and reassures her by instilling hope and reinforcing her faith through prayer and consecrated olive oil.

In Ariana's case the healer gives a detailed explanation as to why she is experiencing her current problems and reassures her by touching various areas of her body such as her hand, back and head. She explains:

> She took out something and she sey [says], "It look like some people trying to do something to you." It look like some De Laurence powers them trying on mi [they are trying on me]; and mi say alright [and I said alright]. God can do everything. God powerful, you know. And she seh mi not to worry [and she says I am not to worry], and she keep on looking on the something. It was a round thing with some colours on it. And she took something out of mi [my] belly . . . glove with powder. Boy mi a tell you [Boy I am telling you], mi nuh know what did happen [I am not sure what had happened]; she just use the lime and then mi see [I saw] the glove with powder coming out so. She give me medication which was in the room. She have a big church you know, and she have a room, and she give me the medicine and she say I must go up and get the bath and then me can go home [and then I can go home]. I felt better after I drink the bush medicine, cause is bush medicine. Me nuh really believe innah the bath though [I do not really believe in the bath though]. Yea. I love the bush medicine.

With some of the misfortunes that Ariana had experienced in life such as not being able to take her exam, losing money, and so on, it made sense when the healer was able to confirm her belief that individuals were using spirits to harm her. The use of the work of De Laurence, the strongest of the evil spirits, showed how much these individuals wanted to harm her. Ariana, however, showed not only her faith in God but also his power to redeem her from this evil. The healer confirmed her belief that God is powerful, which helped to reduce her fears.

Ariana noticed the healer's curiosity when examining the work of De Laurence, by the attention she gave to this round colourful thing that she removed. The healer moved to her belly, and this time she had to use lime to remove a glove with powder. Ariana was able to witness this object coming from within her. She gives a description of the healer's practice, where there was a room with medication and a big church. It is important for her to highlight that the healer had not just any church, but a "big" one, which seemed to confirm that her practices were good. In addition to rubbing her with lime to remove objects from her body, the healer gave her bush medicine and a bath.

Ariana evaluates the treatment she received informing me that the bush medicine is good. However, she says that the bath is not in keeping with her belief system. I wondered if her pointing out the use of church, while not believing in some of the works of the healer, was based on the questions that the Christian church raised towards these practices. She includes this information:

> I've been to fasting and so on at the churches, and one lady told me that my mother is the cause of my sickness because she has done something wrong in the past; that was the faith healer. . . . She say they want me to eat out of garbage bin but the faith healers know the churches. The churches that I go to they tell me that some people at the church told me that my mother did something wrong. She is sorry about it but she doesn't want to tell me about it; and the lady at the hospital, Port Alfredo hospital that I tell you, pray for me. And she say she know my mother and she went up to her one day and say release me of what you do. And she seh if my mother answered her she don't know is when; cause she did something wrong in life and she don't want to accept it. She must release me. My niece grow up now, big, and become Christian; and my niece went to her and told her to release me too; stop allowing the devil to have a leash on me, to have a hold on me . . . and she don't do it. She say she is a Christian and my father is dead and she have a man sleeping with her [in] the night, and is a whole heap of things.

Ariana has been engaging in her spiritual rituals such as visits to different churches and fasting, so as to cope with her problems. It is understandable, given her religious beliefs and the point at which she is at in seeking answers, in addition to the conflict she has experienced with her mother, that it would be natural to accept the information that this lady from the "church" has given her. This information is confirmed by the faith healer. Inasmuch as the need for others to harm her seems feasible, the overriding issue is that her mother is the one causing the problem. Beneath the anger, it seems as though Ariana believes that her mother loves her. The other church members and niece seemed to care about her, as they were willing to go to her mother to plead her case. Again, the theme of right and wrong resurfaces. Ariana indicates that from her credible sources, her mother has done something wrong. Doing what is wrong aligns her with the devil, and to be able to be released from the devil means that she would give someone else to the devil instead of herself. Ariana shows that mother and niece are also Christians. However, she is not convinced that her mother is a Christian as she has disrespected the relationship she had with her father, among other things that she was too angry to discuss.

Charlotte's situation is somewhat different as she relates:

> My mother decided to bring a priest and I said OK, fine. Bring a priest. And it didn't work, because the priest was not . . . I didn't even think he was a Catholic priest, so it was just not gonna work. So I just told her let me just get some holy water. I'll do it myself; and I did it myself and it worked. . . . All the negative energy completely magically disappeared. I mean it was . . . it was really wonderful to see that I wasn't crazy. . . . I am not crazy. I am a Catholic that believe in God and I believe in the power of the Holy Spirit. I believe in the power of the holy water just like Father Albert, just like Father Ho Lung . . . just like all the priest and the nuns in the convent. I used to want to be a nun too. I think like a nun; I think like a priest.

Charlotte's mother was compliant, trying to accommodate her beliefs. Despite her efforts to do so, it seemed as though her mother did not take into consideration her Catholic faith, and brought a priest of a different faith. This illustrates Charlotte's belief in the power of the Catholics, as their priests were seen as being even more powerful than those of another religion. Using the holy water and her Catholic faith, she was able to get rid of negative energy. She takes pleasure in showing that her method worked, which revealed that she was not "crazy" and that there had been the presence of negative energy which she was able to make disappear. There is some mystery to her work, magic in her work, which speaks to how powerful she can be. Charlotte shows that her identity, which had much to do with her Catholic faith, and more specifically her abilities, places her in the category of priests and nuns. She gives the impression that only special individuals are able to use the holy water, as it only works when used by nuns and priests – the very same people with whom she strongly identifies.

Fiona speaks to the power of the healer having knowledge of her situation before she was able to speak of this: "As mi go so the man tell mi say is spirit [when I went to the man, he told me it was spirit]; she don't want anything happen to you [she does not want anything to happen to you]. Is you mother and you stepfather [It is your mother and your stepfather]; you mother don't want to do you anything [your mother does not want anything to do you anything] – the mother love, you know – and him bathe mi down and set mi free [and he gave me a bath and set me free]; set mi [me] free in the name of Jesus. Him set mi [me] free."

Knowing that her mother cares for her seems to bring closure and comfort, this again attests to the African values of maintaining good social relationships. In addition, there is knowledge of good spirits and bad spirits which seem to be battling in their own world. There is indication that spirits can be bad or good, and that there is the spiritual world that protects the living. The healer's use of the bath causes freedom for her. Her gratitude is expressed through her cry to Jesus and a reflection of how important her religious faith is, especially in challenging times.

Thomas indicates that the earlier you know of the spirits the better the prognosis is:

> And a gentleman over the other side see when the spirit them go inside me and never tell me [And a gentleman over the other side saw when the spirits went inside of me and he never told me]. Three years after one of mi little friend hear about this [Three years later one of my little friends heard about this], and tell me [and told me]; if me did hear this from long time me woulddah go to the spiritual people from long time [if I had heard about this from the beginning, I would have gone to the spiritual people from the beginning] and get better healing faster, than to bring me to church and knock out myself. . . . Yeah, [19]97 falling light came down from the sky as a warning and lick mi and shock mi nerves [Yeah, in 1997 a falling light came down from the sky as a warning and hit me and shook my nerves]. People say is a [it is a] falling angel but the devil can transform himself into different things, you know. Yeah. So is the devil. . . . Well she use the olive oil anoint me and spin me round a tree [spun me around a tree] and tell me to mash some cream soda bottle at me home to run weh the spirits [and told me to break some bottles of cream soda at my home to get rid of the spirits].

The mere fact that the other man saw the spirits go into him and did not say anything to Thomas, but rather told someone else, is seen as significant. Maybe it could be that he was afraid of telling Thomas because the spirit was in Thomas. He makes a distinction between the faith healing and the church, the implication being that the faith healers are more powerful than the "church people". The date is significant for Thomas. He associates the sky with angels, but the mere fact that the angel has fallen means it must be the devil. He shared this with others who were able to give him information. Light falling from the sky hit him and affected his nerves. He speaks about the use of rituals such as the use of olive oil, being spun around a tree and breaking the bottle of cream soda when he went home. There is indication that the spirits were at his house also, so when the healer got rid of the spirits from within him, she also had to remove them from his house.

SPIRITS

A consistent theme is the participants' belief that the supernatural is the cause of their mental illnesses, and each participant gives a detailed account of how they believe the spirits have affected them.

Dre describes how powerless he is in the face of spirits:

> I wasn't in control of myself. I would like not just think stuff; it would be a reality in some sense if I think about taking the knife and just poke my eyes out. I would not think it would just happen. That's why I tried hanging myself; it would just happen. My mother came and cut the rope. I went back in the tree and tie it up and jump out and the tree limb tear off. And so other people came and they held me and they were there praying and stuff. I felt imprisoned within my body. I felt like I was fighting to stay inside my body.

He speaks to the power of his thoughts and its interconnection with reality. Dre gives the impression that while examining his thoughts and thinking that these were mere thoughts, he was in fact acting out in reality. His thoughts were his reality. I note that throughout his description his aims were self-destructive, and there were numerous attempts to kill himself. This did not make sense to other individuals who attempted to keep him safe. Dre mentions the support that he received from others who prayed for him and held him close during his suffering. He speaks of the body as a container for him, the disconnection he felt with his body and his need to feel connected. He gives the impression that while he was trying to destroy his body, he was fighting hard to keep himself safe. All of this was out of his control.

Noel had a similar experience:

> I would feel a certain – I would not say personality – but I would feel a certain feeling, like I would hear myself cursing at God but it would not really be me. And then it would worry me; and then I would say to myself, "Wow, was that really me?" And now I would be in trouble with God for doing that. And then I would get frighten and then I would have all the delusions about going to hell; and after that I heard my brain saying things that I was not in control of, you know what I mean? Like really scary stuff.

It is difficult for Noel to admit that the voice he hears cursing at God is his, and that he is unable to stop this from happening. There seems to be a separation when it comes to his experiences, in that one part of him becomes this person who fights against God and has his own personality and feelings, while the other side of him is righteous and would never do something like that. Another part of him examines the conflict that has arisen between these two opposing personalities. The one that goes against God is not congruent with Noel's definition of himself. It goes against everything he stands for, including his being a God-fearing individual. At the same time, he cannot refute that the voice he is hearing is his. This results in him facing reality and being scared of the repercussions of his actions.

Charlotte also made an attempt for me to understand her spiritual experience: "It's, um, just like I know God exist and I can feel God sometimes in my presence . . . I feel it; the air is thick. The air here is thin; it flows well. The air in my house was thick and stifling and I almost wanted to cough. It was the devil." She is saying that you do not necessarily have to see something to know that it is there; you can feel it. She tries to make me understand by making a comparison with her faith in God. She cannot see him, but she knows he is there because she can feel his presence. In the same way, she can sense the type of air that is around her and how it can impact on her well-being. Air that is thin and flows well is considered to be healthy and good air. Air that is thick and stagnant is suffocating for her, targeting the very thing that she needs to live. She makes me become aware of her physical response, and notes that this must be the work of the devil.

Thomas believes that he too has been impacted by the devil. Unlike Charlotte who could sense the spirit of the devil outside and around her, Thomas says that the devil was inside of him:

> The reason why me find myself get weak is because the spirit get inside of me [the reason why I found myself become weak is because of the spirit that got inside of me]. . . . You know with the spiritual world that seems to be green dragon but him nah mek me see him face [but he does not allow me to see his face] is the devil. Is [there are] two dragon – one green one and one red one. When me tell people them nuh believe me still [when I mention it to people, they do not believe me at all]. See normally when me get crazy sometime me get vex it mek [sometimes I will get upset and it makes me] me feel strong, very sad and mi [my] eyes get red.

Thomas attributes his physical energy, its strength or lack thereof, to the spirits possessing him. He lets me know that the spirits that possess him are not good spirits – they are spirits of the devil. He is able to recognize their colours and knows that it is the devil in the form of dragons. But there is still more mystery, as he is unable to see the devil's face. It seems as though he keeps his face hidden, and Thomas has the need to see what he looks like. Thomas wants me to understand the degree of his strength, the tenacity of what he experiences, as not only are there two dragons but they are also the devil. Therefore, when he responds by becoming strong, angry or sad, I should recognize that this is the work of the devil.

With reference to the research questions, I now explore the participants' experiences to determine the causes of their illness, the treatments received, their evaluation of their treatments and how they cope with these, as a guide for drawing conceptual maps of their mental illnesses.

HOW DO PATIENTS CONCEPTUALIZE THEIR OWN MENTAL ILLNESS?

In reviewing each case – Charlotte, Dre, Noel, Ariana, Fiona and Thomas – I examine the following:

- the impact on their illnesses on self;
- the evaluation of the illnesses from two opposing worldviews;
- the ways in which both worldviews address the illnesses; and
- the participants' evaluation of this, which is based on their ability to cope with the given interventions.

Each review is further substantiated by the individual conceptual maps.

Charlotte

Charlotte views herself as a creative, positive individual who enjoys dancing, painting and writing. She assesses that her creativity is disrupted by her home environment, in particular the presence of her sister, who Charlotte believes is a negative person with negative energy, which has affected her positive energy and prevents her from expressing her creativity. She is of the opinion that she can get rid of the negative energy in her home if she is able to have a person who has special spiritual ability bless her house with holy water and prayer. If she can perform this ritual, she will be better able to cope with the situation and will regain her creativity.

In the Western setting, however, Charlotte's beliefs are categorized as a symptom of her mental disorder and she is labelled as a paranoid schizophrenic. Additionally, the Western setting prevents her from accessing her rituals, resulting in her experiencing more distress and difficulty coping. Charlotte's map (figure 3) delineates her illness conceptualization and that of her practitioners' along with its impact on her ability to cope with her illness.

Noel

Noel sees himself as a Christian who has strong religious beliefs. He reveres God and acts according to God's teachings. He is therefore surprised when he hears himself cursing at and disrespecting God, and has become preoccupied with a fear that bad things are going to happen to him; that he is going to be punished by God, become blind, or be taken over by the devil. Unlike Charlotte, Noel believes that he has no control over these fears, and experiences severe distress. He seeks an alternative that is outside of his scope and in this case, it is a psychiatrist.

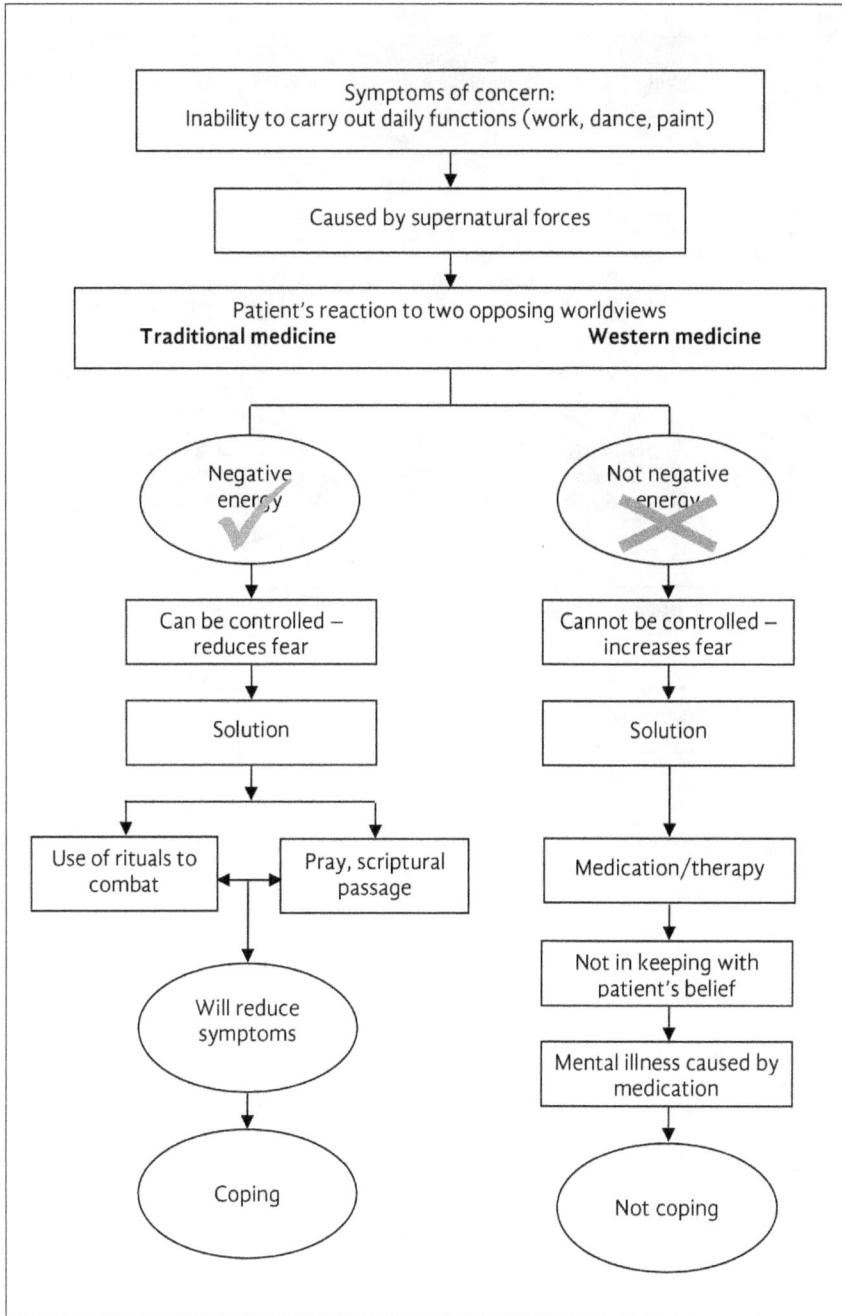

Figure 3. Charlotte's conceptual diagram

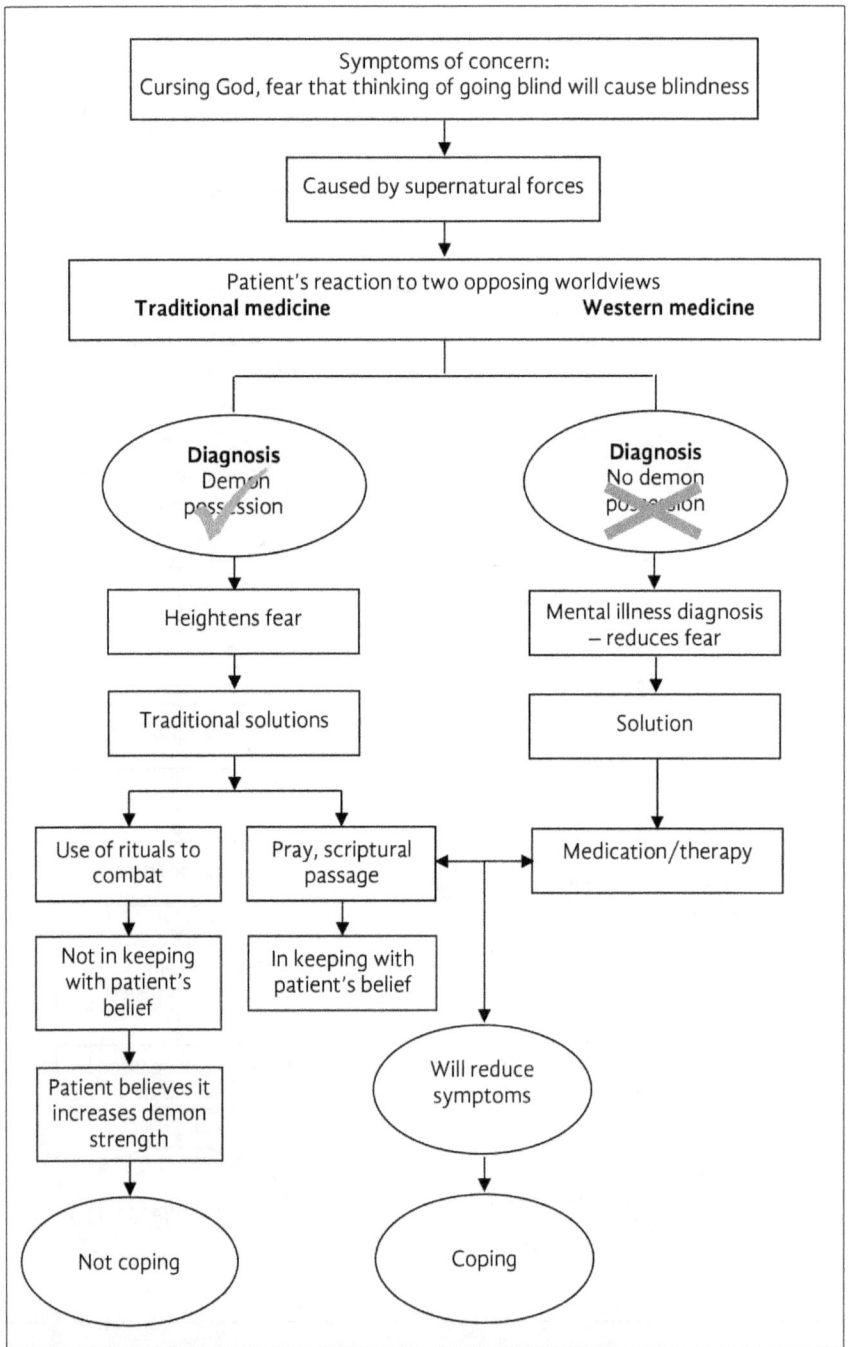

Figure 4. Noel's conceptual diagram

The psychiatrist's explanation of Noel's problem being a mental illness means that Noel is not inherently trying to be disrespectful. The diagnosis of a mental illness helps Noel to be better able to cope with his situation. In addition to getting help from Western medicine, Noel also incorporates his faith (prayer and reading his Bible). Noel's map (figure 4) delineates his illness conceptualization and that of his practitioners' along with its impact on his ability to cope with his illness.

Fiona

Fiona sees herself as a caring mother who ensures the safety and well-being of her children, even her unborn child. Fiona believes that she is faced with two problems – the attack of spirits; and nerve problems. In the first instance, her belief that spirits are trying to harm her baby has resulted in her seeking help from traditional practitioners to get rid of them. Her self-diagnosis, as well as her perception of the type of treatment she should receive, guides her to visit three traditional practitioners before she is able to find the most suitable and effective one.

Although the first one was able to confirm Fiona's belief, the treatment administered did not fully match what Fiona had in mind and was therefore not long lasting – perhaps because it only involved herbal treatment. This led her to the second traditional healer, whose diagnosis was not in keeping with Fiona's, hence the treatment did not work. The third was the best option, as he both confirmed her self-diagnosis and incorporated spiritual and herbal treatment, which she believed she should have initially received. Addressing the spiritual problem allowed Fiona to be able to seek help from Western medicine to address her second concern – nervous tremors. She accepts the Western practitioner's diagnosis and is able to better cope with the situation. Fiona's map (figure 5) delineates her illness conceptualization and those of her practitioners' along with its impact on her ability to cope with her illness.

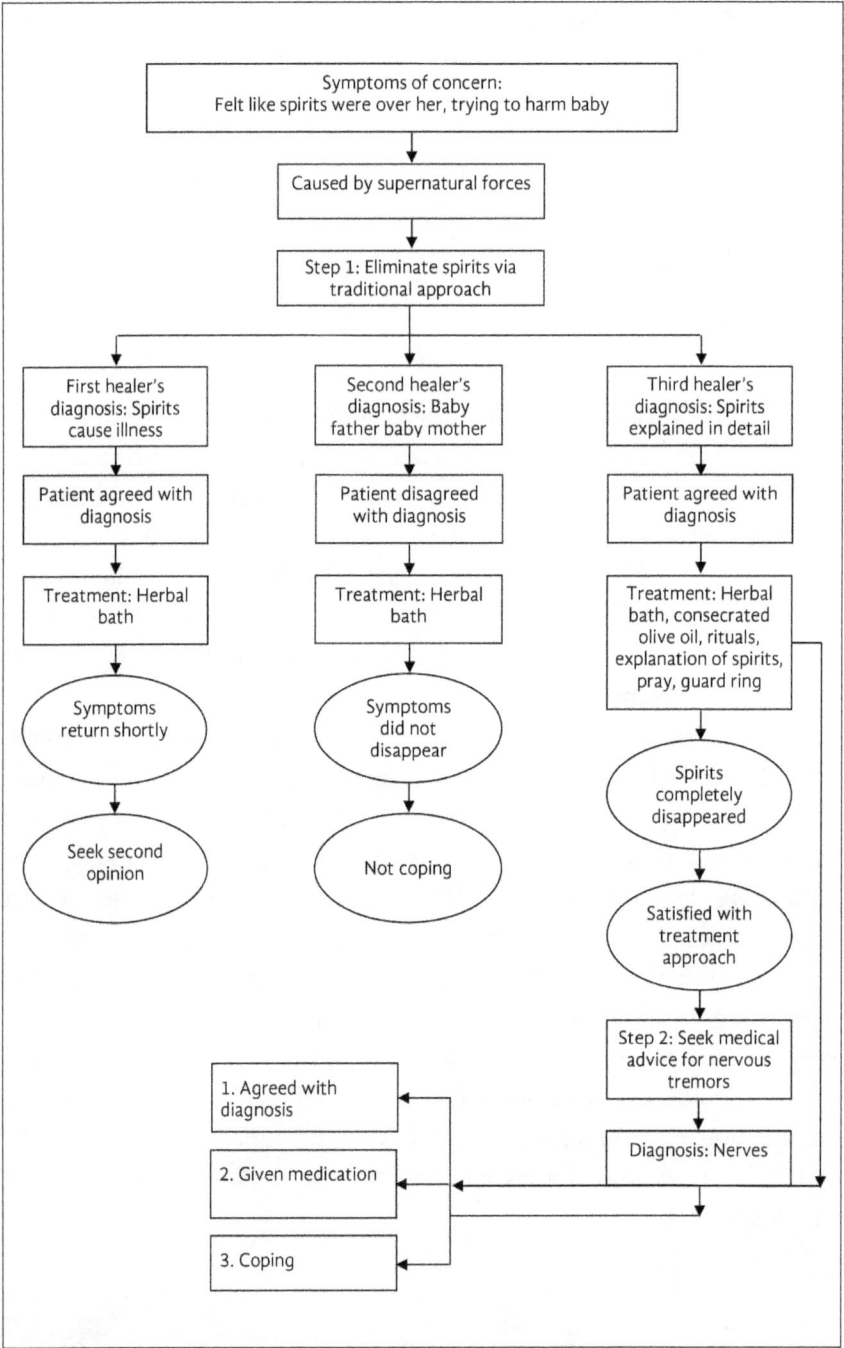

Figure 5. Fiona's conceptual diagram

Dre

Dre considers himself to be a spiritual individual that God has ordained with spiritual gifts to help society to move towards prosperity. He believes that this has made him become prone to spiritual attacks by the devil, who tries to prevent him from fulfilling his purpose. In the Western setting, Dre confides in Western practitioners who, according to him, diagnose him as being paranoid schizophrenic. He disagrees with this diagnosis but continues to receive treatment from Western medicine. He explains that he uses Western medicine to treat the external "physical scars" of his internal spiritual warfare with the devil. In addition to Western medicines' treatment, he also incorporates prayer and rituals, spiritual treatment which helps him to cope with his spiritual warfare. Dre's map (figure 6) delineates his illness conceptualization and that of his practitioners' along with its impact on his ability to cope with his illness.

Ariana

Ariana describes herself as an intelligent nurse and also a loving wife, mother and sister. She believes that she could have been more successful had it not been for others being envious of her intelligence and therefore placing spirits on her. When she was a child her father took her to the first traditional practitioner who gave her a guard ring, which resulted in the termination of her relationship with her then boyfriend. As an adult, she is able to confide in a family member who is a traditional healer. The healer confirmed Ariana's childhood belief that others were trying to use spirits to harm her. She agreed to traditional healing and was then better able to cope with the situation.

In the Western setting, Ariana is faced with what she believes is a hyperactive thyroid which causes her chemical imbalance. This places her in a vulnerable position which allows others to try to put spirits on her. In the psychiatric setting, she tries to protect herself from spirits by requesting her oils, but her request is denied. After initially resisting the medication given, she was eventually able to comply under the guise that her mental illness was caused by hyperthyroidism. In addition to taking her medication, she

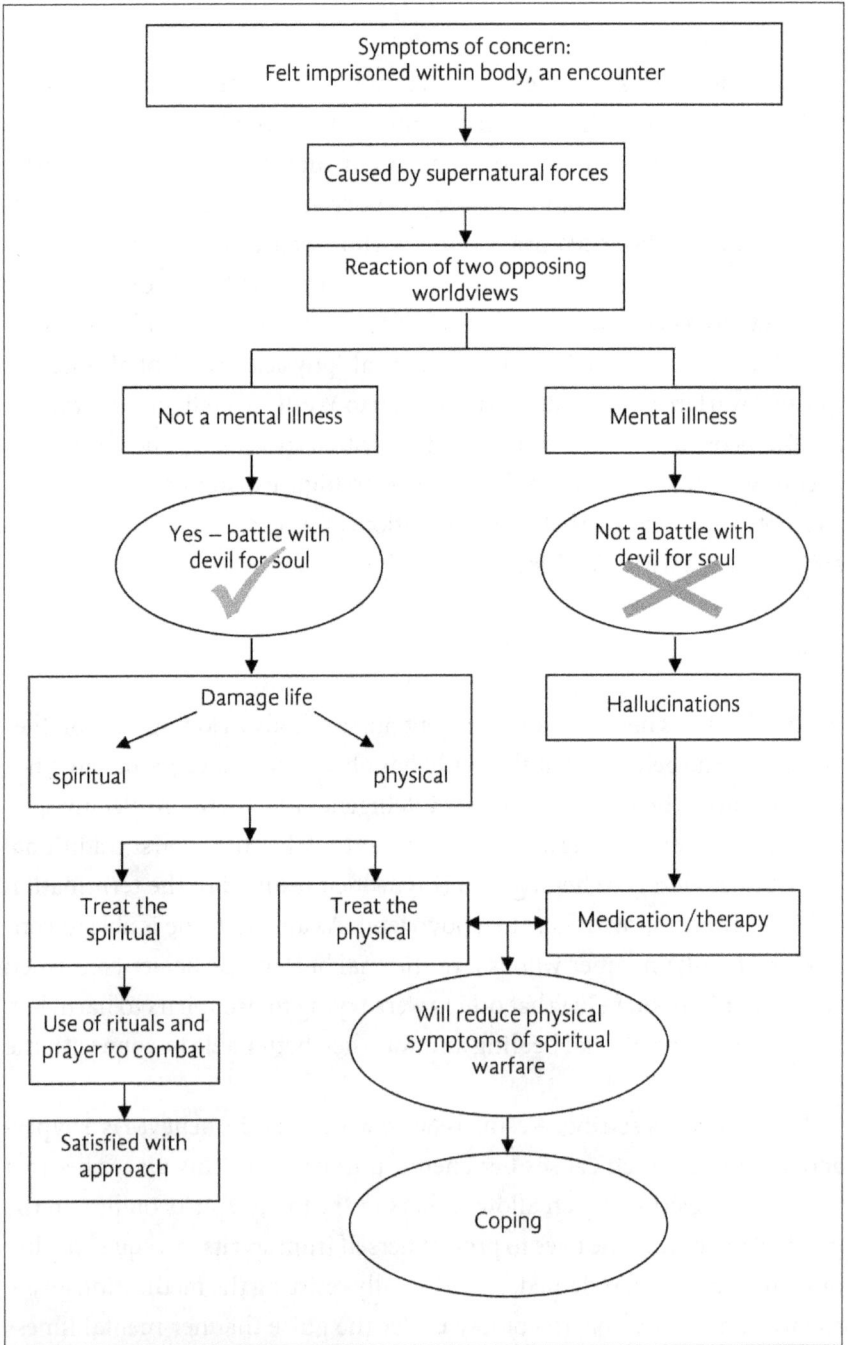

Figure 6. Dre's conceptual diagram

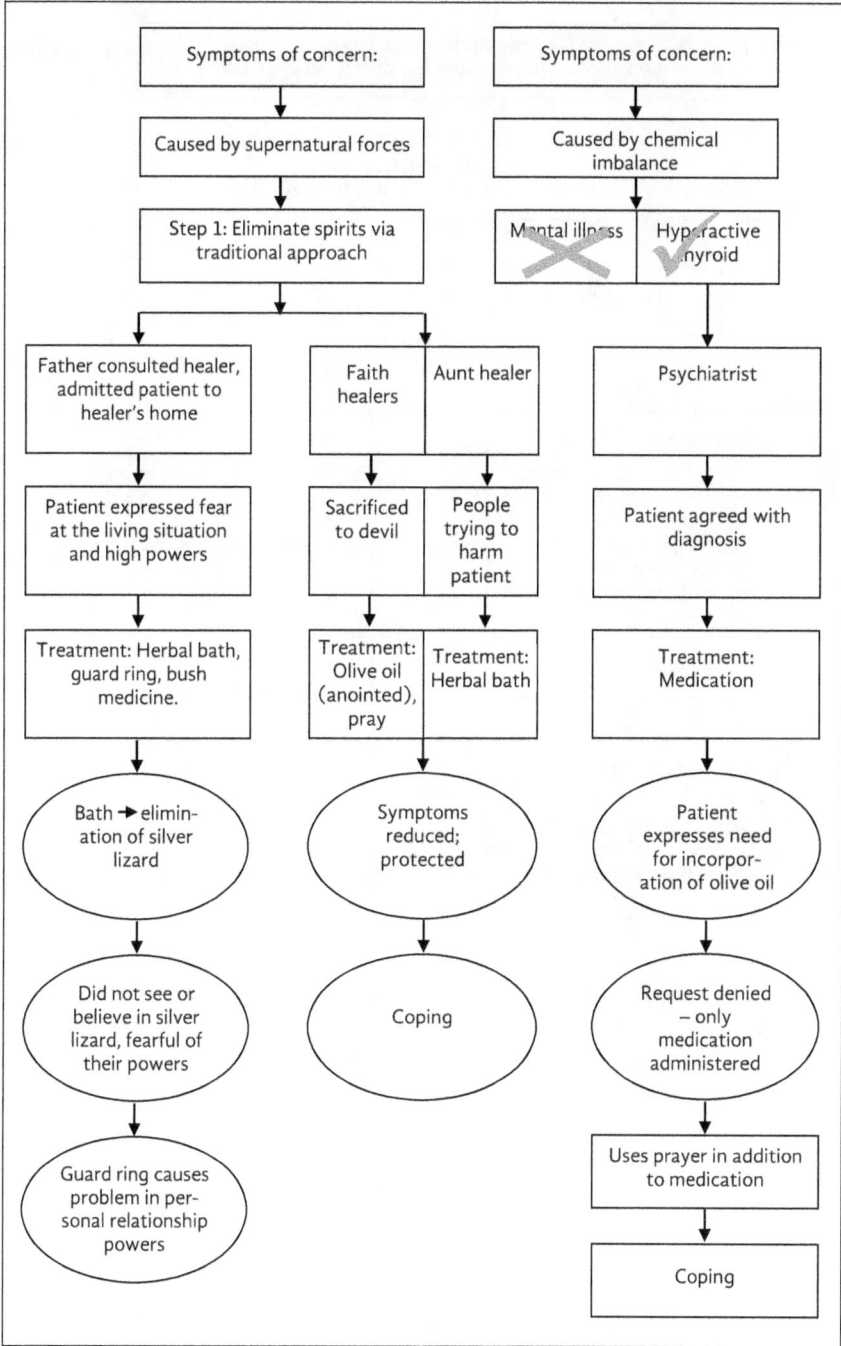

Figure 7. Ariana's conceptual diagram

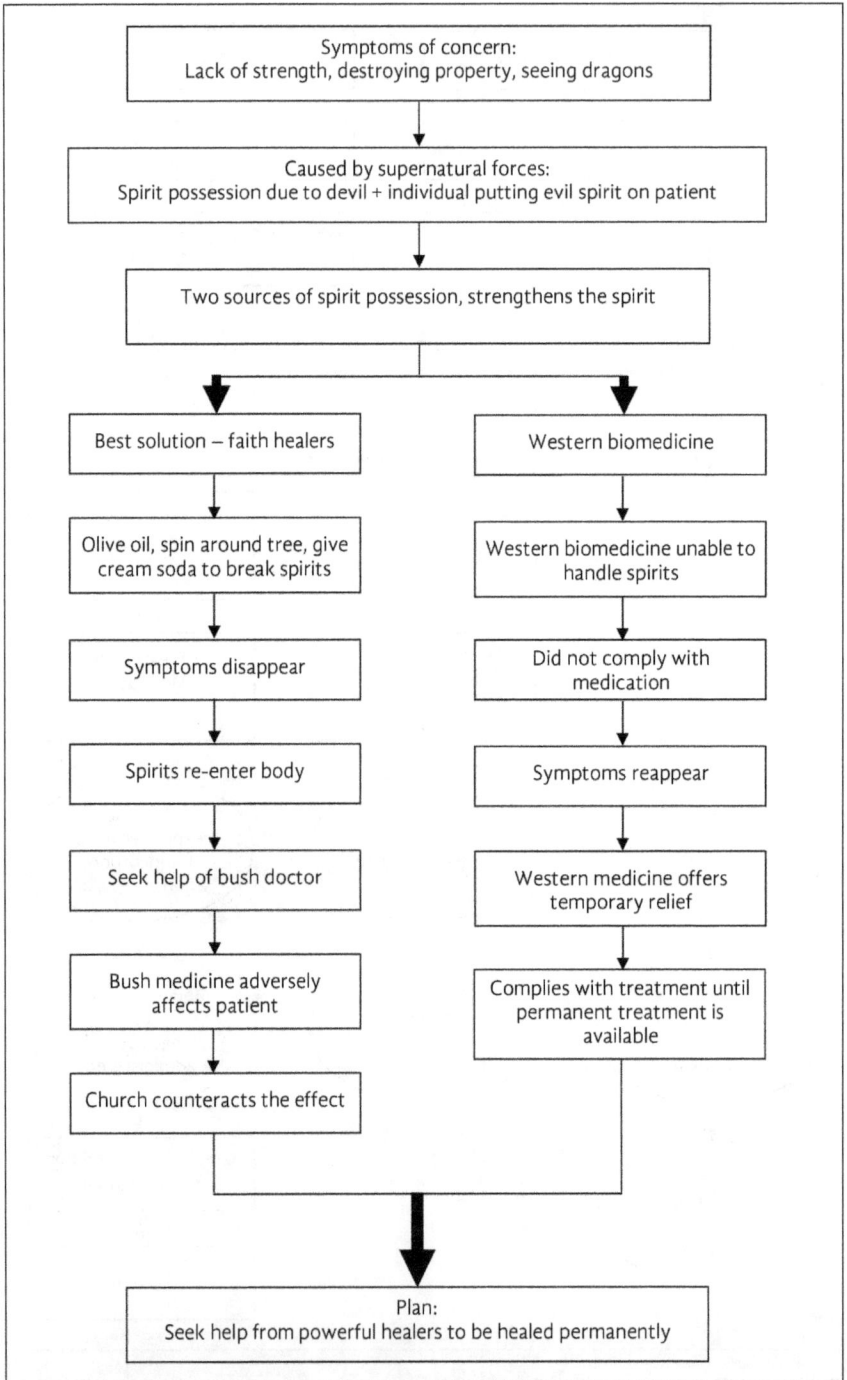

Figure 8. Thomas's conceptual diagram

incorporates prayer, which she believes works best with the medication, and she is able to cope with her situation. Ariana's map (figure 7) delineates her illness conceptualization and those of her practitioners' along with its impact on her ability to cope with her illness.

Thomas

Thomas describes himself as an adventurous person who is determined to find gold in his search for treasure. His desire for material possessions has led to him being attacked by two different sources of spirits. The intensity of his spiritual attack makes him believe that he needs the best traditional healer who can relieve him of these spiritual attacks. According to Thomas, the most effective traditional healers can be found in Antigua, and they are the only ones who can heal him. For the time being, he seeks help from both Western and traditional medicine in Jamaica.

Initially, Thomas seeks help from Western medicine but believes the spirits are too strong; so he discontinues use of the medication and the symptoms from the spirits reappear. He goes to his first traditional healer who helps temporarily, as the spirits re-enter his body. A second traditional practitioner, a herbalist whom he believes is not effective, causes him to suffer from severe side effects of the herbs. He therefore tries to combine both traditional spiritual healing from the church and Western medicine, as he believes that this is the most effective treatment until he is able to go to Antigua in order to get help from the most powerful healers. He is able to cope with his current plan. Thomas's map (figure 8) delineates his illness conceptualization and those of his practitioners' along with its impact on his ability to cope with his illness.

SUMMARY

The participants each recognized some negative change in their behaviour and had made their own diagnosis and prognosis of the problem. This guided the choice in the treatment sought. All six believed at some point, that their illness was caused by the supernatural, and for the most part, chose to incorporate spiritual healing as a means of coping with their problems. They were able to shed light on how the illness takes hold of their sense of self and the fears associated with them trying to make sense and regain control.

It is important to note that when practitioners had a diagnosis similar to that of the participant, the participant was satisfied with the treatment. On the other hand, incongruence between practitioner and patient diagnosis led to not only dissatisfaction, but more psychological distress on the part of the patient. The level of distress of participants tends to decrease when their religious beliefs and rituals are incorporated into their treatment.

CHAPTER 6

....

Meeting the Participant,
Not the Diagnosis

I FINALLY FEEL AS IF I HAVE MET Charlotte, Noel, Dre, Ariana, Fiona and Thomas outside of the psychiatric diagnosis. I am happy to have had the opportunity to meet with each participant in this study. This, coupled with the hermeneutic approach, has brought to me not only a deeper but also a renewed understanding of who they are. In this process I am able to examine my own training and my "self" in the context of the psychiatric setting. It is in comparing my preconceived notions with the transcripts of the patients that I have gained my own insight and arrived at the essences of the experience. I feel that if I am to achieve anything from this research process it would be my relationship with all six participants. As a result, my lifeworld, my "everydayness", has expanded to look beyond the diagnosis and to get to know the person living in this diagnosis.

Scheyett and McCarthy (2006) see narrative therapies as placing more emphasis on viewing the person as separate from and more than their mental health problems. I have learned that when Charlotte is not being "mad" that she is at home doing her paintings, writing and dancing. Thomas likes going out with friends and he is very passionate about his physical possessions. His interest is in finding historical island treasure dating back to the days of slavery. Ariana, the nurse practitioner, is a devoted wife, sister and Christian. She takes care of the household and represents the backbone of the family. Dre is a spiritual man whose aim is to be spiritually mature so as to have an impact on the lives of many. Noel works in the family business. He is a devoted Christian, who is compassionate towards individuals who are going through a difficult time. He reads a lot of psychology, not only to help himself but also to help others. Finally, Fiona is a housewife who shows concern for her children and their wellbeing. She tries to be helpful around the house even in times when she is unable to be.

If I were to say that I had met four "paranoid schizophrenics and two bipolars" it would be inadequate for painting a picture of who these individuals really are. Bochner (2001) encourages an approach of getting to know the patients. He states that when the storied lives of individuals are placed under categories and theories, we miss the essence of what is being told and the treatment process is compromised. Sakalys (2003) suggests that both practitioners and patients can take the journey of understanding this experience where both individuals bring their life stories, intentions, values and history to the interview. With this approach, practitioners no longer guide the patient's account of the illness in the frame of diagnosis; rather they lend an empathetic ear to gain meaning of the phenomenon as experienced by the patient.

Having the advantage of the dual role, being both researcher and practitioner, was a useful tool for me. I found my experience was similar to that of Mak and Elwyn (2003) as the dual role of researcher-practitioner provided continual reflective practice which refined the researcher-practitioner into a craft of communicating with compassion. I began this process by looking at the patients and eventually looked at myself as a part of the interaction with the patient. My reflection on myself and then on the relationship has led me to erase certain blind spots that would aid me in seeing more clearly the impact that I have in listening to the stories of the participants. Mak and Elwyn go on further to state that this dual role has resulted in their finding more depth as well as multiple perspectives, as the phenomenon was not confined to the biomedical model of the disease but presented the person as a whole individual. The research itself allowed the intertwining of various perspectives to create "an embroidery of a whole picture" (400).

I had been criticizing Western biomedical practices without realizing that I, too, formed part of this group of practitioners. It is through the reflective practice of the research process that I have been able to uncover my own self as practitioner and to bracket my preconceptions of both practitioners and patients. In revisiting my morning routine on the wards, this came home to me very clearly. I too am a practitioner. Though I cannot represent all practitioners, I can give voice to this practitioner and I begin to ask the question, am I as disconnected as the practitioners I describe? Surely I do not treat patients as less than a person by ignoring their desire to speak about the supernatural in their psychiatric experience? My training has taught me to be objective and it is this objectivity that will aid in the treatment of the patients. This approach from outside the patient's perspective might seem ineffective but it can be powerful when coupled with more person-centred approaches. For instance, in treatment, Noel was able to function better when he understood that what he was experiencing was a mental disorder as opposed to the work of the devil. Charlotte with her medication adjustment was able to once more experience positive energy. Fiona was able to care for her newborn baby and complete her house chores. Dre was able to allow us to take care of his physical scars and consistently comes to treatment. Ariana felt well enough to go to church and Thomas was able to be compliant in taking his medication as he waited for the opportunity to visit the traditional healers in Antigua.

In showing that the biomedical treatment is working for patients, I am not negating patient concerns about the treatment they receive. Rather, what I would like to suggest is that there is room for improvement in already helpful approaches.

The context in which this study took place was important, as it was only within this "total institution" that I was able to gain deeper understanding into the worldview of each participant. Each of these renewed insights is depicted in figure 9.

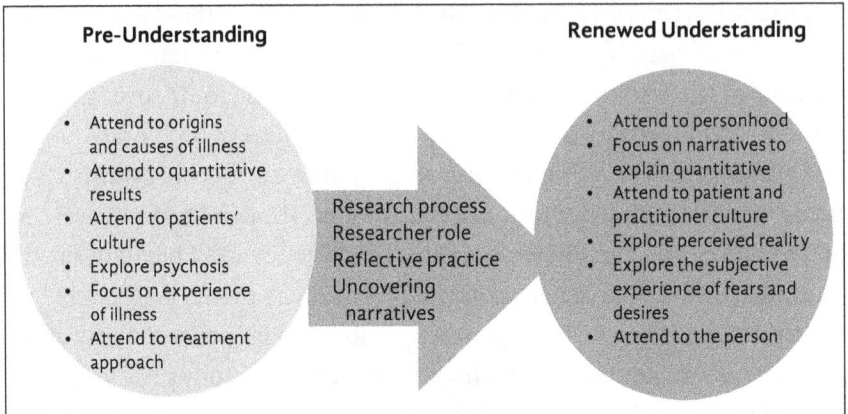

Figure 9. A journey from pre- to renewed understanding

THE ESSENCES

The journey with my fellow-travellers yielded five different essences, each of which is discussed here. Participants consistently showed their attempts to get rid of the label of being mentally ill and to display their individuality and personhood. In spite of their efforts, society has held them captive with the expectation that they would continue to play the role of mentally ill, while neglecting to value instances where they displayed normal behaviour. Unlike physical illness that does not describe the patient – I am "canceric" – the mentally ill person is permanently labelled – I am schizophrenic. The essence underlying the label of a psychiatric diagnosis is a *feeling of entrapment.*

For the most part, despite their conditions, each of the participants has informed me that they have noted changes in their ability to function in their daily lives, whether caused supernaturally, psychologically or physically. Noting their inability to function marked the initial stage of their process of self-diagnosis, which would later determine the mode of treatment they perceived would best address their problem. Contrary to Western practitioners' belief in the lack of insight expressed by psychiatric patients, it seems as though from the onset, patients have had insight into their condition and have been active in regaining normality in their lives. The process of diagnosis and treatment begins before meeting with the practitioner. Participants for the most part, who believe that their illness is supernatural in origin, tend to disagree with the diagnosis given by the Western practitioner. The essence derived from this is that participants *self-diagnose and this may not concur with biomedical diagnosis.*

Participants, in diagnosing their problem, came to one of two conclusions – that the illness was related to supernatural, or to natural causes. For the most part, participants tended to diagnose the problem as supernatural, and in this regard, spiritual treatment was deemed necessary. Some participants also spoke of the spiritual impacting on the physical, and therefore, there was the need to integrate both Western methods to treat the physical, and the traditional to treat the spiritual. Participants of this study saw a state of normality as not only involving the mental and the physical but also the spiritual. Therefore, the essence is *a state of normality, which takes a holistic view of the self, incorporating the mental, physical and spiritual.*

The thought processes are extremely important in mental well-being; more so they are specifically tied to religion. Participants revealed that focusing on negative thoughts could be the gateway for evil spirits (source Satan) entering the psyche and causing harm to the individual, which is expressed as a mental illness. On the other hand, focusing on good thoughts and prosperity equated to God. The most important thing in overcoming evil was to be firmly rooted in belief in God, in good thoughts. The underlying essence in this case is that *thoughts bring about reality.*

In their attempt to claim their sense of self, participants showed where the supernatural, the unseen and ritualistic behaviours were an important part of self-discovery. Some of the rituals seen dated back to the times of slavery. It seems as though participants, in defining who they were, held on to their history and practices of the past in defining their values, beliefs and worldviews. Additionally, they showed that the spiritual dimension was an important part of self, which was maintained by the rituals. In essence, *the supernatural, unseen and rituals are an important part of self.*

The patients' worldview contained the self, the social and historical which impacted on how they perceived their experience. These different facets impacted on the essences that are drawn from this study. A discussion of the general themes that emerged could bring further understanding to how I understand the patient's experiences, worldviews and their essences.

ACKNOWLEDGING PERSONHOOD

When patients enter the psychiatric ward, they each bring with them their own sense of self, their feelings, fantasies, expectations, beliefs and perceptions. Essentially, they bring with them their own stories. This sense of self is dismissed or challenged when viewed through the lenses of psychiatry. The stories are shaped and reshaped within the cultural setting of the ward. In the process of the psychiatric diagnosis, it is difficult to acknowledge the individual's sense of self (James et al. 2013, 254). Throughout the process of this study, each participant introduced me to who they were. For example, Dre described himself as "a purpose driven, flawless, confident person", while Noel described himself as "a very loving, gentle person". For each participant, the need to highlight personal traits took precedence over the psychiatric diagnosis.

Goffman (1959) describes the psychiatric setting as one that is strict, formally organized, rationally planned and in which the individual is expected to play the role of being mentally ill. While not negating the fact that the psychiatric institution impacts on the individual by virtue of these expectations, the findings of this study indicate that psychiatric patients are not passive in their treatment but that they also have their own set of expectations of the psychiatric institution. One of these expectations is the need to acknowledge the person behind the diagnosis, noting their uniqueness and individuality.

JUST BECAUSE I BELIEVE IN GOD DOES NOT MAKE ME A SCHIZOPHRENIC

Sayre (2000) discusses the concerns of medical practitioners with regard to psychiatric patients' response to hospitalization, which often is met with resistance to the idea of being ill, and a refusal to comply with treatment. Psychiatric patients' inability to recognize that they suffer from severe mental illness and are in need of psychiatric care may be perceived by the practitioner as lack of insight. This is seen as a result of the cognitive deficit due to the mental illness. It is therefore not uncommon for the practitioner to see patients' resistance as being a part of the psychosis and therefore meaningless. In an effort to help get patients back into society and functioning once more, the practitioner may start the treatment process without acknowledging what the patients are saying.

It is in this regard that the patients reported that the conversation that they had with the practitioner, including twelve of the sixty patients stated, "He does the talking, I do the listening"; and "I can't speak to him. He does not listen/understand." The comments made by the patients confirm how practitioners' techniques are viewed as removing the patient from the treatment process. Further, patients have revealed that one of the most painful and dehumanizing aspects of living with their diagnosis was the loss of their personal identity when labelled with a mental illness (Schyett and McCarthy 2006). The process of diagnosis and hospitalization also seeks to reinforce what Hatfield and Lefley (1993) refer to as the patients' sense of failure. Gold (2007) encourages practitioners not to ignore patients' stories but to use them as a means of bonding, and of providing support and care for the person. Thomas, Bracken and Leudar (2004) further reiterate that the psychoses shared by our patients are very meaningful and in addition to being aware, we should also be empathetic. It is when we utilize these methods that we transform the health-care system into a healing system.

In hearing the voices of the participants, I noted that the theme of oppression was born out of us, as practitioners, not listening to the patients, and while we are taught not to entertain these "mad stories", when I took the opportunity to listen, I was able to uncover more about each participant. Charlotte, in rejecting her diagnosis, was stating that she had a strong belief in God and in negative and positive energy. Noel was saying that he was afraid of disappointing God and getting into trouble with Him. Dre was saying that he had had encounters with something supernatural. All this information provided useful insight and knowledge into the patients' perception of what they believed to be the causes of their experience of illness.

The question then, for us as practitioners, is, "How can we ask patients for insight into the problem when their experience has been construed in a story form that is not being heard?" It is clear that had we listened to these stories, we would realize that the patients were actually sharing their insight. Charlotte was aware that the negative energy did not allow her to paint anymore. Dre was unable to become spiritually mature. Noel was unable to return to school and socialize. In gaining insight, we as practitioners should be more flexible and acknowledge that a change has occurred; that that is not how one normally functions and so get help. The patients all took this approach. They may or may not have attributed what they experienced to mental illness; however, they were able to acknowledge the loss of a previous lived experience. The only difference between what patients have said and the medical model is the use of the term "mental illness".

RELIGION

In the Caribbean, we had ties with our African religious heritage long before the introduction of Western biomedicine. That heritage is therefore endemic to the larger culture and to the individual. A large proportion of how participants conceptualized their illness had to do with the supernatural world. More than two-thirds of the quantitative sample believed that someone could perform Obeah. The effects of the supernatural continued to be a pervasive theme throughout the results, as it related to participants' reasons for their illness and for seeking treatment. Culturally, Jamaica is described as a religious society. Rowe and Allen (2004) suggest that the spiritual dimension forms an integral part of the individual's worldview. It is this dimension that conditions the person's interpretation, comprehension and reaction to life experiences. This would explain why often the participants' initial reaction was to turn to their religious faith in the face of their illness. Additionally, it seems as though the participants' definition of health also incorporated a spiritual component (Hamilton 1998) by virtue of thinking that Satan caused illness and God was the solution. Griffith (1983) further highlights the importance of treating the individual as a whole person; taking into account the spirit, mind and body. Three spheres (spirit, mind and body) are critical to holistic care. One may go further to add that perhaps health, as proposed by the World Health Organization, should also consider including the spiritual dimension in its definition.

Socially, we can see where "spiritual health" is a strong part of and is active in the Jamaican culture. For instance, in Noel's account he showed where the teachers were praying for him to ward off the devil. Charlotte spoke of her mother bringing a priest to bless the house, and Fiona said that the community had also been seeing the ghosts of her mother and stepfather and she was encouraged to use a guard ring to protect her baby. The religious practices such as laying on of hands and praying, noted by researchers such as Wedenoja and Griffith in 1983, are still reported by the participants as being practised by their healers. Wedenoja also acknowledges that these groups provided psychological support for the patients. It therefore stands to reason that it is not unusual to seek religious refuge when faced with problems. Western biomedicine ignores the religious component; however, the underlying concept is the same. Western practitioners Ellis and MacLaren (2005) and Beck (1972) speak about the individual's thoughts causing their behaviours. The participants also spoke to this. For instance, Fiona showed anxiety in talking about evil spirits, and noted that her anxiety was reduced when the healer mentioned to her that God would take care of everything. If the underlying concept is the same from the perspective of both Western medicine and the participants, in understanding how thoughts can affect behaviour, how then can we move forward to work with patients on this common ground?

I often wonder what the patients did differently with the traditional practitioner. Other than the mystery of his methods, the participants seemed to be more welcoming of his approach. Perhaps one of the answers as to how to move ahead lies in examining the reports given of the traditional practitioner. I have noted various reactions from patients regarding their experiences with the traditional practitioner when compared with the Western practitioner. The discussions with the traditional practitioner entailed the practitioner explaining the nature of the problem and the patients telling them everything about their experiences of the problem. It seems that the patient tends to have more input, and receives a fuller explanation from the traditional practitioner. Healy and Jaspers (1990, 1965 as cited in Sayre 2000) have both examined the biomedical approach that we normally take in our treatment and they believe that we have placed too much emphasis on labelling the psychosis, suggesting instead that we should turn our attention to understanding the psychotic experience as it gives us a more accurate understanding of the patients.

Although the participants in this study provided information on their interaction with the traditional practitioner which seemed to be beneficial to them, the quantitative results show that Western practitioners are not open to patients utilizing this mode of treatment as the traditional practitioners are viewed in a negative light. Of the three approaches, traditional healing, traditional herbalist and alternative medicine, alternative medicine seemed to receive more positive reviews than the others. This is understandable, given that alternative medicine is closer to the practice of Western medicine and is widely accepted as a method of treatment. Perhaps Caribbean Western-trained practitioners are influenced by our own respected Caribbean psychiatrists, such as Beaubrun (1966), who warn practitioners against incorporating traditional medicine into Western practices (see chapter 2). Although participants in my study have not indicated experiencing harm from using traditional medicine, there are studies that indicate that in some instances it can have tremendous negative impact (Dein 1997). On the other hand, some practitioners have acknowledged patients' interest in utilizing traditional medicine and have agreed that if that were subjected to scientific scrutiny, they would be more inclined to accept it as a possible treatment option.

CLINICAL PRACTICALITY OF HERMENEUTIC PHENOMENOLOGY

When practitioners engage in dialogue with patients only to confirm a psychiatric diagnosis, they rob themselves and the patient of the opportunity to share in the lived experience of the patient. This "medicalized psychiatric" approach (Aho and Guignon 2011, 293) is often criticized as limiting the nature and quality of the relationship between practitioner and patient, resulting in the patients feeling disconnected, having a sense of defeat and lacking agency in their recovery process. Hermeneutic phenomenology, although used primarily as a research methodology in this book, has been shown to be an effective method in this "dialogical exchange" (Aho and Guignon 2011, 298) which has resulted in a deep, rich understanding of patient experiences.

The first contribution that this approach has is with *transforming the nature of practitioner-patient dialogue*. Though each of these patients' experiences has a unique dimension, there are commonalities found among each. This approach sheds light on the identity of the patient, the importance of their beliefs and religion, their social relationships, the meanings they attribute to their mental illness as well as what matters to them. When practitioners engage with patients, it is important for them to consider the qualities of each patient. Acknowledgement of this allows for the patient to feel recognized and helps to improve on the quality of the relationship between practitioners and their patients.

The second practicality that hermeneutic phenomenology brings to clinical practice is *spending more time with the person and less time with the diagnosis.* The more patients realize that practitioners see them as individuals, the more they will be trusting of our intentions towards them. Through their narratives, patients have brought to our awareness the two different worldviews (the Western biomedical and the traditional) that they encounter and how they manage both. These narratives bring into context the historical events from colonialism that seem to be playing out in our interactions with our patients. Given that research has shown evidence of a strong colonial influence on our current institutions, Western practitioners should be mindful that they are not engaging with the patients in a manner that is reflective of the colonial past. One such example is employing measures which may prevent the patients from expressing their African retention. This requires that we as practitioners take into account the cultural context of our Western schooling and what that may mean for a patient whose worldview entails traditional beliefs. This level of awareness can be the first step in us developing a more open relationship with our patients.

In order to get at these *truths,* practitioners need to become more aware of themselves and their own narratives. This level of awareness will impact the amount and quality of the information that patients divulge. The third contribution, therefore, is to *recognize our own training and our own biases and become more aware of how we choose to engage with our patients.* Do we want to, for instance, bring to our patients the notion that we are discounting their worldviews by firmly positioning ours? Or do we want to use an approach that allows us to efficiently serve our patients by allowing them to share what matters to them?

Indeed, this social and linguistic encounter between the practitioner and the patient results in the patient getting a sense of and being caught up in the practitioner's way of being; together they both form a "single intersubjective situation" (Aho and Guignon 2011, 300). The patients therefore become perceptive of and reflect how the practitioners receive their narrative and how caring or attentive they are to the process. Thus, if practitioners demonstrate openness, appear to be non-judgemental, and are willing to listen and understand, patients will in turn become more open to disclosure. An added bonus here, is that while the patient is sharing and the practitioner is listening, the patient will also sense that the practitioner's self is one that is more stable when compared to the "chaotic" nature of the patient's narrative (Aho and Guignon 2011, 300). This stable sense of being presented by the practitioner will bring some reassurance and safety to the patient.

The fourth contribution is *to transform the previous narratives that the patients have of us.* Let it no longer be one where the patients express that we, the practitioners are not engaged – "they don't listen; they don't understand" – to a narrative of becoming actively present. This transformation would offer patients some amount of necessary stability through their difficult time.

As human beings we are situated in a world of meanings, where we also make our own meanings. The meaning we make will guide our sense of agency and how we position ourselves in our worlds. If patients believe that the psychiatric approach focuses only on the physical and there is no room to share their own notions, especially if it is considered non-physical, then their sense of agency becomes diminished. The fifth contribution is *to give patients the opportunity to share their own meaning.* While we can suggest our treatment approaches and the meaning we make of their experiences, we need to recognize that this is only one perspective and that patients may have other perspectives which they believe is also helpful. Our approach to methods other than our own needs to be re-examined.

Lastly, when a story is shared with and received by another individual, it increases the connection between the storyteller and the receiver. In this process of hermeneutic phenomenology, I have illustrated patients' willingness to share with me their thoughts and fears, even those that are frightening. The fact that they were able to have this space for a conversation may have served as an opportunity to provide them with more insight into understanding their situation. The sixth contribution is, therefore, *to recognize the impact of receiving.* Receiving the stories that our patients bring to us can have a profound effect on the therapeutic relationship that we have with our patients. The traditional practitioners are ahead of us in this dimension as patients seem to believe that they are more receptive to listen to their stories than are the Western practitioners.

CONCLUSION AND RECOMMENDATION

The journey I actually took in this study was nothing like the one I initially expected. I began with sixty psychiatric patients, counting spirits in an effort to understand their illness narratives and reliance on traditional medicine. The more spirits I counted, the more I realized that the numbers could not tell me what the quality of the relationship between Western medicine and traditional medicine was from a patient perspective. My journey took a different path at this point, slowing down to meet and understand my fellow-travellers on the psychiatric wards, no longer moving so quickly that all I could do was count spirits. For me, hermeneutic phenomenology took me closer towards my desire to understand patients' worldviews, although my limited scope of their engagement with Western and traditional medicine has now widened to encompass a deeper understanding of Charlotte, Noel, Dre, Ariana, Fiona and Thomas. In my journey, I have learned to reflect on my role as a practitioner and to go beyond its usual definitions. I have learned to gain an understanding of what living in the world of an individual who is mentally ill means, and the struggle to reveal and define personhood as it relates to these patients. The purpose of this study is to introduce others to the process that I have been through to reach to this level of understanding. My preconceived notions have been replaced with renewed thinking that I am sure will once again be challenged when I get back to my "everydayness". Nevertheless, through this study, I would like us as practitioners to examine and evaluate our relationships with our patients. My appreciation for my training in Western medicine is more valuable to me in light of what I now know about the complementarity of both opposing worldviews.

With this in mind the following recommendations are offered. As practitioners we should use *intentionality* to examine our *everydayness*. Often we go about our daily activities without noticing the information that lies beyond the walls of the psychiatric setting. Valuing of awareness and being in tune with the setting can give us more understanding of the patients' experiences, while allowing us to be more empathetic. If we are to put ourselves in the positions of our patients, then we can start to deconstruct the label of a diagnosis and start to focus on the person. We can treat people, not illnesses. As mentioned earlier in this study, one of the themes that emerged from the patient interviews is the need to establish their individuality. If we are to take into consideration the person, the social environment, the culture and the history, we can have a more person-centred approach that honours the personhood of both patient and practitioner within the total institution.

My approach as a fellow-traveller taught me that for me to treat patients I have to trust that they are the experts in their illness. Asking them to take my hand and allowing me to see through their lenses creates a trusting bond of mutual respect. The power dynamics of the practitioner as knower and the patient as passive are relinquished. It requires a sense of togetherness. Yes, we are the experts in treating the illness, but the patients are also the experts in the experience itself. Instead of simply building an efficient case for treatment, we can gain an understanding of who the individual is and appreciate the person that is larger than the illness. We move beyond the psychosis to the person, to their lived experiences.

Much of what I have learned and understood could not have been made possible without the narratives of these participants. The time that each took to explain to me what their experiences were like is more memorable than any textbook representation that I have ever had. I therefore recommend that we take time with the patients and let them share their stories, as these provide powerful information.

In this study, the emphasis was placed mainly on the patient participants and less on the practitioners. For the purpose of future studies, the storied lives of the practitioners as it relates to the psychiatric setting could be an area to examine. A strong theme emerged of the supernatural as the cause of illness, leading to seeking help from the traditional practitioner. Whereas the patients seemed to evaluate the traditional practitioners positively, we are not clear on how effective these practices are in bringing about psychological health. Despite the Obeah Act, patients are still seeking help from the traditional practitioners. Although other researchers such as Wedenoja, Beaubrun, Royes, Hickling, Weaver and Griffith have started the process, there is still a paucity in the literature for the Caribbean.

References

Acemoglu, Daron, Simon Johnson and James A. Robinson. 2001. "The Colonial Origins of Comparative Development: An Empirical Investigation". *American Economic Review* 91:1369–401. https://doi.org/10.3386/w7771.

Adame, Alexander L., and Gail A. Hornstein. 2006. "Representing Madness: How Are Subjective Experiences of Emotional Distress Presented in First-Person Accounts?" *Humanistic Psychologist* 34, no. 2: 135–58. https://doi.org/10.1207/s15473333thp3402_3.

Aho, Kevin, and Charles Guignon. 2011. "Medicalized Psychiatry and the Talking Cure: A Hermeneutic Intervention". *Human Studies* 34, no. 3: 293. https://doi.org/10.1007/s10746-011-9192-y.

Allport, Gordon W. 1940. "The Psychologist's Frame of Reference". *Psychological Bulletin* 37, no. 1: 1–28.

Amador, Xavier F., David H. Strauss, Scott A. Yale and Jack M. Gorman. 1991. "Awareness of Illness in Schizophrenia". *Schizophrenia Bulletin* 17, no. 1: 113–32. https://doi.org/10.1093/schbul/17.1.113.

American Psychiatric Association. 2000. *Diagnostic and Statistical Manual of Mental Disorders*. 4th ed. Washington, DC: American Psychiatric Association.

Barrett, Robert. 1998. "The Schizophrenic and the Liminal Persona in Modern Society". *Culture, Medicine and Psychiatry* 22, no. 4: 465–94. https://doi.org/10.1023/a:1005393632053.

Beaubrun, Michael H. 1966. "Psychiatric Education for the Caribbean". *West Indian Medical Journal* 15:52–62.

Beck, Aaron. 1972. *Depression: Causes and Treatment*. Philadelphia: University of Pennsylvania Press.

Benson, Herbert. 1996. *Timeless Healing: The Power of Biology and Belief.* New York: Scribner.

Bochner, Arthur P. 2001. "Narrative's Virtues". *Qualitative Inquiry* 7, no. 2: 131–57. https://doi.org/10.1177/107780040100700201.

Bruce, Judith C. 2002. "Marrying Modern Health Practices and Technology with Traditional Practices: Issues for the African Continent". *International Nursing Review* 40, no. 3: 161–67. https://doi.org/10.1046/j.1466-7657.2002.00109.x.

Cassidy, F.G., and R.B. Le Page, eds. 2002. *Dictionary of Jamaican English*. 2nd ed. Kingston: University of West Indies Press.

Cocks, Michelle, and Valerie Møller. 2002. "Use of Indigenous and Indigenised Medicines to Enhance Personal Well-Being: A South African Case Study". *Social Science and Medicine* 54, no. 3: 387-97. https://doi.org/10.1016/S0277-9536(01)00037-5.

Cohen, Marlene Zichi, David L. Khan and Richard H. Steeves. 2000. *Hermeneutic Phenomenological Research: A Practical Guide for Nurse Researchers*. Thousand Oaks, CA: Sage.

Corin, Ellen, and Ciles Bibeau. 1980. "Psychiatric Perspectives in Africa. Part II: The Traditional Viewpoint". *Transcultural Psychiatry* 17, no. 4: 205-43. https://doi.org/10.1177/136346158001700401.

Cottle, Thomas J. 2002. "On Narratives and the Sense of Self". *Qualitative Inquiry* 8, no. 5: 535-49. https://doi.org/10.1177/107780002237003.

Council on Scientific Affairs. 1999. "Neonatal Circumcision". http://www.ama-assn.org/ama/pub/category/1810.html.

Crawford, Tanya, and Maurice Lipsedge. 2004. "Seeking Help for Psychological Distress: The Interface of Zulu Traditional Healing and Western Biomedicine". *Mental Health, Religion and Culture* 7, no. 2: 131-48. https://doi.org/10.1080/13674670310001602463.

Daniels, Victor. 2005. "Lecture on Phenomenology". http://web.sonoma.edu/users/d/daniels/phenomlect.html.

Dein, Simon. 1997. "ABC of Mental Health: Mental Health in a Multiethnic Society". *British Medical Journal* 315, no. 7106: 473-76. https://doi.org/10.1136/bmj.315.7106.473.

Eatough, Virginia, and Jonathan A. Smith. 2017. "Interpretative Phenomenological Analysis". In *Sage Handbook of Qualitative Research in Psychology*, edited by Carla Willig and Wendy Stainton-Rogers, 193-211. London: Sage.

Edwards, Stephen David. 1986. "Traditional and Modern Medicine in South Africa: A Research Study". *Social Science and Medicine* 22, no. 11: 1273-76. https://doi.org/10.1016/0277-9536(86)90194-2.

Edwards, Stephen David, Pieter W. Grobbellar, V.N. Makunga, Patrick Themba Sibaya, Louis M. Nene, Stanley T. Kunene and S.A. Magwaza. 1983. "Traditional Zulu Theories of Illness in Psychiatric Patients". *Journal of Social Psychology* 121, no. 2: 213-21. https://doi.org/10.1177/107780002237003.

Ellis, Albert, and Catharine MacClaren. 2005. *Rational Emotive Behavior Therapy: A Therapist's Guide*. 2nd ed. Atascadero, CA: Impact.

Ellison, Christopher G., and Jeffrey S. Levin. 1998. "The Religion-Health Connection: Evidence, Theory, and Future Directions". *Health Education and Behaviour* 25, no. 6: 700-720. https://doi.org/10.1177/109019819802500603.

Encyclopedia of the Nations. 2007. "Jamaica: Country Overview". http://www
.nationsencyclopedia.com/Americas/Jamaica-ETHNIC-GROUPS.html.

Engebretson, Joan. 1994. "Folk Healing and Biomedicine: Culture Clash or Complementary Approach?" *Journal of Holistic Nursing* 12, no. 3: 240–50. https://doi.org
/10.1177/089801019401200303.

Erinosho, Olayiwola, A. 1976. "Notes on the Concept of Disease and Illness: The
Case of the Yoruba, Nigeria". *Nigerian Journal of Economic and Social Studies*
18, no. 3: 471–75.

Eskin, Mehmet. 1989. "Rural Population's Opinions About the Causes of Mental
Illness: Modern Psychiatric Help – Sources and Traditional Healers in Turkey".
International Journal of Social Psychiatry 35, no. 4: 324–28. https://doi.org/10.1177
/002076408903500404.

Fraser, Heather. 2004. "Doing Narrative Research: Analysing Personal Stories
Line by Line". *Qualitative Social Work* 3, no. 2: 179–201. https://doi.org/10.1177
/1473325004043383.

Gallagher, Eugene B. 1976. "Line of Reconstruction and Extension in the Parsonian
Sociology of Illness". *Social Science and Medicine* 10, no. 5: 207–18. https://doi.org
/10.1177/1473325004043383.

Goffman, Ervin. 1959. "The Moral Career of the Mental Patient". *Psychiatry* 22, no.
2: 123–42. https://doi.org/10.1080/00332747.1959.11023166.

Gold, Elizabeth. 2007. "From Narrative Wreckage to Islands of Clarity: Stories of
Recovery from Psychosis". *Canadian Family Physician* 53, no. 8: 1271–75.

Goode, D. Tawara, and Sharonlyn Harrison. 2000. "Policy Brief 3: Cultural
Competence in Primary Health Care. Partnerships for a Research Agenda".
Georgetown University Child Development Center, National Center for Cultural
Competence, Washington, DC.

Greene, Jennifer C., Valerie J. Caracelli and Wendy F. Graham. 1989. "Toward a
Conceptual Framework for Mixed-Method Evaluation Designs". *Educational
Evaluation and Policy Analysis* 11, no. 3: 255–74. https://doi.org/10.3102%2F01623
737011003255.

Griffith, Ezra E. 1983. "The Significance of Ritual in a Church-Based Healing Model".
American Journal of Psychiatry 140, no. 5: 568–72.

Groleau, Danielle, Alan Young and Laurence J. Kirmayer. 2006. "McGill Illness
Narrative Interview (Mini): An Interview Scheduled to Elicit Meanings and
Modes of Reasoning Related to Illness Experience". *Transcultural Psychiatry*
43, no. 4: 671–91. https://doi.org/10.1177/1363461506070796.

Hamilton, David G. 1998. "Believing in Patients' Belief: Physician Attunement to
the Spiritual Dimension as a Positive Factor in Patient Healing and Health".

American Journal of Hospice and Palliative Medicine 15, no. 5: 276–79. https://doi.org/10.1177/104990919801500509.

Harper, David, and Andrew R. Thompson. 2012. *Qualitative Research Methods in Mental Health and Psychotherapy: A Guide for Students and Practitioners*, edited by David Harper and Andrew R. Thompson, 1–8. Malden, MA: Wiley-Blackwell.

Hatfield, Agnes B., and Harriet P. Lefley. 1993. *Surviving Mental Illness: Stress, Coping, and Adaptation*. New York: Guilford Press.

Hayes, Mark, and Ethan Watrall. 2000. *The Asclepion*. Bloomington: Indiana University.

Hickling, Frederick W. 1975. "Psychiatric Care in a General Hospital Unit in Jamaica". *West Indian Medical Journal* 24, no. 2: 635–37.

———. 1989. "Sociodrama in the Rehabilitation of Chronic Mentally Ill Patients". *Psychiatric Services* 40, no. 4: 402–6. https://doi.org/10.1176/ps.40.4.402.

———. 1993. "Psychiatry in Jamaica: Growth and Development". *International Review of Psychiatry* 5, no. 2–3: 193–203. https://doi.org/abs/10.3109/09540269309028310.

———. 2010. "Psychiatry in Jamaica". *International Psychiatry* 7, no. 1: 9–11. https://doi.org/10.1192/S1749367600000928.

———. 2018. "From Explanitions and Madnificent Irations to de Culcha Clash: Popular Theatre as Psychotherapy". *Interventions* 6, no. 1: 45–66. https://doi.org/10.1192/S1749367600000928.

Hickling, Frederick W., and Roger C. Gibson. 2012. "Decolonization of Psychiatric Public Policy in Jamaica". *West Indian Medical Journal* 61, no. 4: 437–41.

Hickling, Frederick W., and Caryl James. 2008. "Traditional Mental Health Practices in Jamaica: On the Phenomenology of Red Eye, Bad-Mind and Obeah". In *Perspectives in Caribbean Psychology*, edited by Frederick W. Hickling, Brigitte K. Matthies, Kai Morgan and Roger C. Gibson, 465–86. London: Jessica Kingsley.

Insel, Kathleen Collins, Paula M. Meek and Howard Leventhal. 2005. "Differences in Illness Representation among Pulmonary Patients and Their Providers". *Journal of Health Psychology* 10, no. 1: 147–52. https://doi.org/10.1177/1359105305048561.

James, Caryl C.B. 2012. "Psychiatric Patients' Evaluation of the Efficacy of Obeah vs. Western Medicine in Treating Their Mental Illness". *Journal of Psychology in Africa* 22, no. 1: 134–38. https://doi.org/10.1080/14330237.2012.10874531

James, Caryl C.A.B., Karen A. Carpenter, Karl Peltzer, and Steve Weaver. 2013. "Valuing Psychiatric Patients' Stories: Belief in and Use of the Supernatural in the Jamaican Psychiatric Setting". *Transcultural Psychiatry* 51, no. 2: 247–63. https://doi.org/10.1177/1363461513503879

James, Caryl C.A.B., and Karl Peltzer. 2012. "Traditional and Alternative Therapy for Mental Illness in Jamaica: Patients' Conceptions and Practitioners'

Attitudes". *African Journal of Traditional, Complementary and Alternative Medicines* 9, no. 1: 94–104. https://doi.org/10.4314/ajtcam.v9i1.14.

Jorm, Anthony F. 2000. "Mental Health Literacy. Public Knowledge and Beliefs about Mental Disorders". *British Journal of Psychiatry* 177, no. 5: 296–401. https://doi.org/10.1192/bjp.177.5.396.

Kiev, Ari. 1963. "Beliefs and Delusions of West Indian Migrants to London". *British Journal of Psychiatry* 109, no. 460: 356–63. https://doi.org/10.1192/bjp.109.460.356.

Kirmayer, Laurence J. 2006. "Beyond the New Cross-Cultural Psychiatry: Cultural Biology, Discursive Psychology and the Ironies of Globalization". *Transcultural Psychiatry* 43, no. 1: 126–44. https://doi.org/10.1177/1363461506061761.

Kleinman. Arthur. 1980. *Patient and Healers in the Context of Culture. An Exploration of the Borderland between Anthropology, Medicine, and Psychiatry.* Vol. 3. Berkeley: University of California Press.

Koltko-Rivera, Mark E. 2004. "The Psychology of Worldviews". *Review of General Psychology* 8, no. 1: 3–58. https://doi.org/10.1037%2F1089-2680.8.1.3.

Kuper, Adam. 1999. "South African Anthropology: An Inside Job". *Paideuma* 45:83–101. https://www.jstor.org/stable/40341765.

Kvale, Steiner. 1996. "InterViews: An Introduction to Qualitative Research Interviewing". Thousand Oaks, CA: Sage.

Larkin, Michael, and Andrew R. Thompson. 2012. "Interpretative Phenomenological Analysis in Mental Health and Psychotherapy Research". In *Qualitative Research Methods in Mental Health and Psychotherapy,* edited by David Harper and Andrew R. Thompson, 101–16. Malden, MA: Wiley-Blackwell. https://doi.org/10.1002/9781119973249.

Leontiev, Dmitry A. 2007. "Approaching Worldview Structure with Ultimate Meanings Technique". *Journal of Humanistic Psychology* 47, no. 2: 243–66. https://doi.org/10.1177%2F0022167806293009.

Leventhal, Howard, Ian Brissette and Elaine A. Leventhal. 2003. "The Common-Sense Model of Self-Regulation of Health and Illness". In *The Self-Regulation of Health and Illness Behaviour,* edited by L.D. Cameron and H. Leventhal, 42–65. New York: Routledge.

Lewis, Aubrey. 1934. "The Psychopathology of Insight". *British Journal of Medical Psychology* 14, no. 4: 332–48. https://doi.org/10.1111/j.2044-8341.1934.tb01129.x.

Lindo, Jascinth, Affette McCaw-Binns, Janet LaGrenade, M. Jackson and Denise Eldemire-Shearer. 2006. "Mental Well-Being of Doctors and Nurses in two Hospitals in Kingston, Jamaica". *West Indian Medical Journal* 55, no. 3: 153–59.

Lopez, Kay A., and Danny G. Willis. 2004. "Descriptive Versus Interpretive Phenomenology: Their Contributions to the Nursing Knowledge". *Qualitative*

Health Research 14, no. 5: 726–35. http://qhr.sagepub.com/cgi/content/abstract/14/5/726.

Mak, Yvonne, and Glyn Elwyn. 2003. "Use of Hermeneutic Research in Understanding the Meaning of Desire for Euthanasia". *Palliative Medicine* 17, no. 5: 395–402. https://doi.org/10.1191/0269216303pm7750a.

Mayoh, Joanne, and Anthony J. Onwuegbuzie. 2015. "Toward a Conceptualization of Mixed Methods Phenomenological Research". *Journal of Mixed Methods Research* 9, no. 1: 91–107. https://doi.org/10.1177%2F1558689813505358.

McClean, Stuart. 2003. "Doctoring the Spirit: Exploring the Use and Meaning of Mimicry and Parody at a Healing Centre in the North of England". *Health* 7, no. 4: 483–500. https://doi.org/10.1177%2F13634593030074006.

Merleau-Ponty, Maurice, and Collin Smith. 2002. *Phenomenology of Perception: An Introduction.* 2nd ed. London: Routledge.

Miller, William R., and Carl E. Thoresen. 2003. "Spirituality, Religion, and Health: An Emerging Research Field". *American Psychologist* 58 no. 1: 24–35. https://doi.org/10.1037/0003-066x.58.1.24.

Ministry of Justice, Jamaica. 2013. Mental Health Act. https://moj.gov.jm/sites/default/files/laws/The%20Mental%20Health%20Act.pdf.

———. Obeah Act. https://moj.gov.jm/sites/default/files/laws/The%20Obeah%20Act.pdf.

Mishler, Elliot G. 2005. "Patient Stories, Narratives of Resistance and the Ethics of Human Care: À la Recherche de Temps Perdu". *Health* 9, no. 4: 431–51. https://doi.org/10.1177/1363459305056412.

Muller, Anton, and Mariana Steyn. 1999. "Culture and the Feasibility of a Partnership between Westernized Medical Practitioners and Traditional Healers". *Society in Transition* 30, no. 2: 142–56. https://doi.org/10.1080/10289852.1999.10520179.

Murray, Michael. 1997. "A Narrative Approach to Health Psychology: Background and Potential". *Journal of Health Psychology* 2, no. 1: 9–20. https://doi.org/10.1177/135910539700200102.

Myers, Gary E. 2002. "Can Illness Narratives Contribute to the Delay in Hospice Admission?" *American Journal of Hospice and Palliative Care* 19, no. 5: 325–30. https://doi.org/10.1177/104990910201900509.

Mzimkulu, Kanyiswa G., and Leickness C. Simbayi. 2006. "Perspectives and Practices of Xhosa-Speaking African Traditional Healers when Managing Psychosis". *International Journal of Disability, Development and Education* 53, no. 4: 417–31. http://dx.doi.org/10.1080/10349120601008563.

Nji, Fokwa J. 2018. "Continuity or Discontinuity of Blessing Rituals in African Traditional Religion: Towards a Contextual Theology of Christian Faith among the *Meta'* People in North West Cameroon". Thesis, South African Theological Seminary.

Nin, Anaïs. 1961. *Seduction of the Minotaur.* Chicago: Swallow Press.

Nunn, Nathan. 2012. "Culture and the Historical Process". *Economic History of Developing Regions* 27, no. sup1: S108–S126. http://dx.doi.org/10.1080/207803 89.2012.664864.

O'Cathain, Alicia, Elizabeth Murphy, and Jon Nicholl. 2007. "Why, and How, Mixed Methods Research Is Undertaken in Health Services Research in England: A Mixed Methods Study". *BMC Health Services Research* 7, no. 85. https://doi .org/10.1186/1472-6963-7-85.

Ogden, Thomas. 1994. *Subjects of Analysis.* Northvale, NJ: Rowman and Littlefield.

Okello, Elialilia S., and Stella Neema. 2007. "Explanatory Models and Help-Seeking Behaviour: Pathways to Psychiatric Care among Patients Admitted for Depression in Mugalo Hospital, Kampala, Uganda". *Qualitative Health Research* 17, no. 1: 14–25. https://doi.org/10.1177/1049732306296433.

Patton, Michael Q. 2001. *Qualitative Research and Evaluation Methods.* Thousand Oaks, CA: Sage.

Peltzer, Karl. 2000. "Perceived Treatment Efficacy of the Last Experienced Illness Episode in a Community Sample in the Northern Province, South Africa". *Curationis* 23, no. 1: 57–60. https://doi.org/10.4102/curationis.v23i1.599.

———. 2001 "An Investigation into the Practices of Traditional and Faith Healers in an Urban Setting in South Africa". *Health SA Gesondheid* 6, no. 2: 3–11. http:// dx.doi.org/10.4102/hsag.v6i2.62.

Peltzer, Karl, and Wielandt Machleidt. 1992. "A Traditional (African) Approach towards the Therapy of Schizophrenia and its Comparison with Western Models". *Therapeutic Communities* 13, no. 4: 229–42.

Pyne-Timothy, Helen. 2002. "(Re) Membering African Religion and Spirituality in the African Diaspora". *Journal of Haitian Studies* 8, no. 1: 134–49.

Razali, S.M., U.A. Khan, and C.I. Hasanah.1996. "Belief in Supernatural Causes of Mental Illness among Malay Patients: Impact on Treatment". *Acta psychiatrica scandinavica* 94, no. 4: 229–33. https://doi.org/10.1111/j.1600-0447.1996.tb09854.x.

Rosenwald, George C., and Richard L. Ochberg. 1992. *Storied Lives: The Cultural Politics of Self-Understanding.* New Haven, CT: Yale University Press.

Rowe, M. Michelle, and Richard G. Allen. 2004. "Spirituality as a Means of Coping with Chronic Illness". *American Journal of Health Studies* 19, no. 1: 62–67.

Royes, K. 1962. "The Incidence and Features of Psychosis in a Caribbean Community". In *Proceedings of the Third World Congress of Psychiatry*, vol. 2, 1121–25. Montreal: University of Toronto Press and McGill University Press.

Sakalys, Jurate A. 2003. "Restoring the Patient's Voice. The Therapeutics of

Illness Narratives". *Journal of Holistic Nursing* 21, no. 3: 228–41. https://doi.org /10.1177%2F0898010103256204.

Sarason, Irwin G., and Barbara R. Sarason. 1999. *Abnormal Psychology: The Problem of Maladaptive Behavior, Study Guide*, 9th ed. Upper Saddle River, NJ: Prentice Hall.

Saravanan, B., A. David, D. Bhugra, M. Prince and K.S. Jacob. 2005. "Insight in People with Psychosis: The Influence of Culture". *International Review of Psychiatry* 17, no. 2: 83–87. https://doi.org/10.1080/09540260500073596.

Sayre, Joan. 2000. "The Patient's Diagnosis: Explanatory Models of Mental Illness". *Qualitative Health Research* 10, no. 1: 71–83. https://doi.org/10.1177 /104973200129118255.

Schyett, Anna M., and Erin McCarthy. 2006. "Men and Women with Mental Illnesses: Voicing Different Service Needs". *Affilia* 21, no. 4: 407–14. https:// doi.org/10.1177/0886109906292114.

Sharif, SA, Gboyeba Ogunbanjo, NH Malete. 2003. "Reasons for Non-Compliance to Treatment among Patients with Psychiatric Illness: A Qualitative Study". *South African Family Practice* 45, no. 4: 10–13. https://doi.org/10.4102/safp.v45i4.1963.

Sheikh, Shaheen, and Adrian Furnham. 2000. "A Cross-Cultural Study of Mental Health Beliefs and Attitudes towards Seeking Professional Help". *Social Psychiatry Psychiatric Epidemiology* 35, no. 7: 326–34. https://doi.org/10.1007/s001270050246.

Siebert, Al. 2000. "How Non-Diagnostic Listening Led to a Rapid "Recovery" from Paranoid Schizophrenia: What Is Wrong with Psychiatry?" *Journal of Humanistic Psychology* 40, no. 1: 34–58. https://psycnet.apa.org/doi/10.1177/0022167800401005.

Simon, Richard C., and Herbert Pardes, eds. 1985. *Understanding Human Behaviour in Health and Illness*, 3rd ed. Philadelphia: Lippincott Williams and Wilkins.

Skott, Carola. 2001. "Caring Narratives and the Strategy of Presence: Narratives Communication in Nursing Practice and Research". *Nursing Science Quarterly* 14, no. 3: 249–54. https://doi.org/10.1177%2F08943180122108364.

Solomon, Robert C. 1989. *From Hegel to Existentialism*. Oxford: Oxford University Press.

Teuton, Joanna, Richard Bentall and Chris Dowrick. 2007. "Conceptualizing Psychosis in Uganda: The Perspective of Indigenous and Religious Healers". *Transcultural Psychiatry* 44, no. 1: 79–114. https://doi.org/10.1177/1363461507074976.

Thomas, Philip, Patrick Bracken and Ivan Leudar. 2004. "Hearing Voices: A Phenomenological-Hermeneutic Approach". *Cognitive Neuropsychiatry* 9, nos. 1–2: 13–23. https://doi.org/10.1080/13546800344000138.

van den Geest, Sjaak. 1997. "Is There a Role for Traditional Medicine in Basic Health Services in Africa? A Plea for a Community Perspective". *Tropical Medicine and International Health* 2, no. 9: 903–11. https://doi.org/10.1046/j.1365-3156.1997 .d01-410.x.

Van Dongen, Els. 2003. "Walking Stories: Narratives of Mental Patients as Magic". *Anthropology and Medicine* 10, no. 2: 207–22. https://doi.org/10.1080/1364847 032000122863.

Waldron, Ingrid. 2010. "The Marginalization of African Indigenous Healing Traditions within Western Medicine: Reconciling Ideological Tensions and Contradictions along the Epistemological Terrain". *Women's Health and Urban Life* 9, no. 1: 50–68.

Wang, Qi, and Jens Brockmeier. 2002. "Autobiographical Remembering as Cultural Practice: Understanding the Interplay between Memory, Self and Culture". *Culture and Psychology* 8, no. 1: 45–64. https://doi.org/10.1177/13540 67X02008001618.

Ward, Tony, and Frederick Hickling. 2004. "Psychology in the English-Speaking Caribbean". *Psychologist* 17, no 8: 442–44.

Weaver, Steve. 2003. "Health and Illness in Rural Community: A Study of Traditional Healthcare Practices in the Parish of St Thomas". PhD diss., University of the West Indies, Mona, Jamaica.

Wedenoja, William. 1983. "Jamaican Psychiatry". *Transcultural Psychiatry, Research Review* 20, no. 4: 233–58. https://doi.org/10.1192/S1749367600000928.

Wedenoja, William Andrew. 1978. "Religion and Adaptation in Rural Jamaica". PhD diss., University of California, San Diego.

Weiss, Mitchell. 1997. "Explanatory Model Interview Catalogue (EMIC): Framework for Comparative Study of Illness". *Transcultural Psychiatry* 34, no. 2: 235–63. https://doi.org/10.1177/136346159703400204.

Wittkower, Eric D. 1970. "Transcultural Psychiatry in the Caribbean: Past, Present and Future". *American Journal of Psychiatry* 127:162–66. https://psycnet.apa.org /doi/10.1176/ajp.127.2.162.

Wojnar, Danuta M., and Kristen M. Swanson. 2007. "Phenomenology an Exploration". *Journal of Holistic Nursing* 25, no. 3: 172–80. https://doi.org/10.1177/089801010 6295172.

WHO (World Health Organization). 1946. "Preamble to the Constitution of the World Health Organization as Adopted by the International Health Conference". New York, 19–22 June, 1946; signed on 22 July 1946 by the representatives of 61 States (Official Records of the WHO, no. 2, p. 100) and entered into force on 7 April 1948.

———. 2009. "WHO-AIMS Report on Mental Health System in Jamaica". WHO and Ministry of Health Jamaica, Kingston, Jamaica.

Wolman, Benjamin B., ed. 1973. *Dictionary of Behavioral Science*. New York: Van Nostrand Reinhold.

Yalom, Irvin D. 2002. *The Gift of Therapy*. New York: HarperCollins.

Index

www.ingramcontent.com/pod-product-compliance
Lightning Source LLC
Chambersburg PA
CBHW030653270326
41929CB00007B/337